Feedsack Secrets

Fashion from Hard Times

By Gloria Nixon

Feedsack Secrets

Fashion from Hard Times

By Gloria Nixon
Edited by Judy Pearlstein
Design by Kelly Ludwig
Photographs by Roger Nixon
Production Assistance by Jo Ann Groves

Published by Kansas City Star Books
1729 Grand Boulevard
Kansas City, Missouri 64108
All rights reserved

Thanks to Gateway Packaging for allowing us to use art from their ad published in *Fortune*, January 1948

First edition, first printing
ISBN: 978-1-935362-31-9
Library of Congress number: 2009943678

Printed in the United States of America
By Walsworth Publishing Co.
Marceline, Missouri

To order copies, call StarInfo, 816-234-4636 (Say "Operator.")
KANSAS CITY STAR BOOKS

www.Pickledish.com http://www.pickledish.com/

The Quilter's Home Page

Table of Contents

Acknowledgements

Many hearts and hands worked together to bring this book to completion. I deeply appreciate the contribution made by each of the following:

The research facilities of Hale Library at Kansas State University were invaluable to this project. Search Specialist, Daniel Ireton, located archived volumes and promptly forwarded details. The entire staff was eager to help, which made my job much easier. Profound thanks are owed to each of them.

Sarah Muirhead, Publisher/Editor with The Miller Publishing Company, gave encouragement as the research began and generously allowed photographs, advertisements, cartoons and articles from past issues of *Feedstuffs* and T*he Northwestern Miller* to be used in *Feedsack Secrets*.

Roger D. Miller, CEO, president and founder of Gateway Packaging Company, enthusiastically supported the book-in-progress and approved the use of quoted material from Percy Kent publications, the photo of Richard K. Peek and the Percy Kent advertisements from Fortune Magazine. Sharon Tuttle, Human Resources Executive at Gateway's Kansas City location, sent two booklets on the history of the Percy Kent Bag Company to aid in research. My sincere thanks to both of you!

Photos from catalogs and references to MONTGOMERY WARD and WARDS are courtesy Midwest Catalog Brands, Inc. MONTGOMERY WARD and WARDS are registered marks of Midwest Catalog Brands, Inc.

Peter Havens, Publisher of *The National Provisioner*, kindly allowed the use of cartoons and ads from *Feeds Illustrated*, including the picture announcement of Susie-Q.

Permission to use the photo of W. Lee O'Daniel and his Hillbilly Band came through the Texas Department of Criminal Justice in Huntsville and the Director of Public Information, Michelle Lyons. John Anderson, Archives Preservation Officer with the Texas State Library & Archives Commission, was instrumental in guiding the request through the proper channels.

Rett Schuler, President of Fulton Denver Company, approved the Fulton Fulprint ads from *Feed Age* and expressed interest in the research.

Bemis Company, Inc., gave permission to use the advertisement introducing the Betty Bemis doll. Kristine Pavletich in Public Relations is due a thank you for handling the request.

The two photos of Chase Pretty Prints and multiwall bags are courtesy of International Paper.

The National Cotton Council of America and the Textile Bag and Packaging Association offered helpful information on vintage cotton bag booklets. Thank you to both organizations and especially to Marjory Walker, NCC Director of Communications, and Maxine Shapiro, Executive Director of TBPA.

Others helped in various ways and are deserving of many thanks:

Marcia Kaylakie brought details about the novelty O'Daniel flour sack to the attention of the quilt history world and was always gracious in answering my questions.

Feedsack historians Christine Motl and Nan Moore lent photographs of the O'Daniel sack to aid in research.

Ruth Rhoades generously shared points from her feedsack research and took the time to answer a number of questions.

Pepper Cory gave a much-needed listening ear when the project was in the early stages.

Cynthia Collier, Joyce Anderson, Susan Wildemuth, Andi Reynolds, Sheryl Till, and Hank and Louise Schelter sent notes of encouragement. They were words at the right time.

A very special thank you is reserved for my family who encouraged the writing of *Feedsack Secrets*. Each one offered loving support for which I will always be grateful.

A heartfelt thank you is given to my husband, Roger, who watched our home change from neat and orderly to one that, at times, was far from it, yet never uttered a word of complaint. Thank you for lightening the load, solving computer problems, taking dozens of feedsack pictures and editing them. I truly could not have done this without you.

Many loving thanks go to my daughter Amy Karsmizki and to Ann Stankewitz, Nellie Scoggins, Freddy Scoggins, Bob Ausbourne and Carolyn Willis.

Not the least in all of these are the staff of *Kansas City Star Quilts*, Kelly Ludwig for her wonderful book design, Jo Ann Groves for production assistance, my editor, Judy Pearlstein, sales and marketing manager, Diane McLendon, who championed the book, and publisher, Doug Weaver. This book would not be possible without your hard work. I humbly thank you for having faith in me.

To each one of you and to all feedsack collectors and enthusiasts, "Thank you!"

Dedication

This book is dedicated to the love of my life, Roger Nixon.

About the Author

Gloria Nixon and her husband Roger live in the Flint Hills of rural Wabaunsee County, Kansas. They enjoy attending local farm auctions where Roger searches for woodworking tools and Gloria keeps an eye open for a feedsack or two. That's how she found her first dress print bags some ten years ago. She also collects *Kansas City Star* patterns and old quilt ephemera.

Gloria is a quilt history researcher who especially enjoys studying individuals and the contribution each made to quilt history. She is a member of the American Quilt Study Group (AQSG), the Iowa Illinois Quilt Study Group (IIQSG) and the Feedsack Memories discussion group. Her articles appear in *Pieces of Time: A Quilt and Textile History Magazine*. This is her first book with *The Kansas City Star*.

Introduction

The purpose of this work is to share recent discoveries in the story of the patterned feedsack, also known as the dress print bag. The account begins in the early 1920s with a young man's invention that grew in popularity to become a national phenomenon. Today, more than eighty years later, interest remains high and has spread around the globe.

Tens of thousands of pages from old farm periodicals, magazines and newspapers were searched for information that might add to our understanding of feedsack history. Volumes untouched for decades and covered in dust were brought from the archives to be examined. Fascinating details emerged and are presented here. It is my sincere hope you enjoy the new things learned about the history of the dress print bag in *Feedsack Secrets: Fashion from Hard Times*.

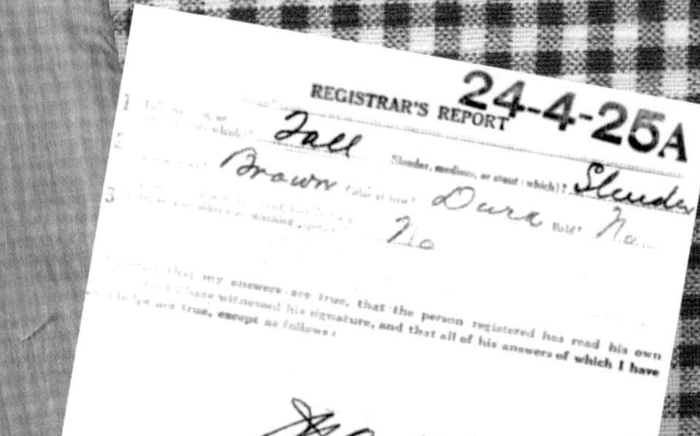
REGISTRAR'S REPORT

24-4-25A

Tall

Slender, medium, or stout (which)? Slender

Brown

Dark

No

No

that my answers are true, that the person registered has read his own

that I have witnessed his signature, and that all of his answers of which I have

knowledge are true, except as follows:

(Signature of registrar)

7 Ward 7

Kansas City.

Missouri.

June 5, 19

(Date of registration)

— Chapter One. —
The Father of the Dress Print Bag

On April 28, 1922, The Washington Post announced, "Farewell to the Old Flour Sack." Big millers thought it a good idea to replace five-pound flour sacks with paper cartons. Cartons would be more convenient to handle and make storage easier for the city housewife. In just a few short years, however, both city and rural housewife would see the old flour sack in a new light. Changes were coming, thanks to a young man named Asa T. Bales.

Asa Theodore Bales was born in Roscoe, Missouri, on July 14, 1892. He was the only child of Alva Jane and Charles H. Bales. In the early 1900s, the Bales family lived in Kansas City, owned a house and had occupations typical of the time. Charles was employed as a streetcar motorman, and Alva worked at home as a seamstress. Seventeen-year-old Asa held the position of salesman in a music store.

The years passed and Asa fell in love with a young woman from Missouri. He and Allene Ballen were married on October 16, 1913. Before the newlyweds could celebrate their first anniversary, the world was embroiled in war. In April of 1917, the United States declared war on Germany and shortly thereafter passed the Selective Service Act, requiring all male citizens between the ages of twenty-one and thirty to register for military service. The few details known about Asa's appearance are written on his military registration card. He is described as tall and

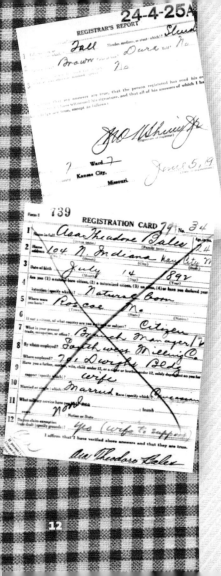

slender with dark hair and brown eyes. His occupation is listed as Branch Manager of Southwest Milling Company.

Allene and Asa had a son in February of 1918. It was undoubtedly a stressful time for the young couple. The war still raged and Asa received notice to report to the Army. He was inducted in late summer and sent to Camp McArthur, Texas, where he served until being discharged.

The following year was not a happy one for Asa and Allene. By the time the January 1920 census was taken, they had separated. Asa was living in his parents' house in Kansas City. The same census lists Allene and baby Robert with her parents in Carroll County, Missouri.

BALES, ASA T.		4,277,632	W
(Surname) (Christian name)		(Army serial number)	(Race)

Residence:

    3818 E 17TH ST KANSAS CITY, MO

(Street and house number)	(Town or City)	(County)	(State)

*Inducted at: **KANSAS CITY** on **9/5/1918**

Place of birth: **ROSCOE, MO**   Age or date of birth: **14JUL1892**

Organizations served in, with dates of assignments and transfers:

    CO F 2 BN DEV BN CAMP MCARTHUR,TX TO DIS

Grades, with date of appointment:

    PVT

Engagements:

Wounds or other injuries received in action:

Served overseas from †   To †   from †   To †

Honorably discharged on demobilization   **Y**

In view of occupation he was, on date of discharge, reported   **N**   per cent disabled

Remarks:

Form No. 724-1, A.G.O.   *Strike out words not applicable. †Dates of departure from and arrival in the U.S.

(top left) Registrar's report with Asa's physical description.
(lower left) Asa T. Bales draft registration card.
(above) Missouri State Archives' World War I service record for Asa T. Bales.

The Invention

World War I was finally over and the country entered the Roaring Twenties. Changes were many and for the better in wages, technology, public health, science, literature and art. It was an exciting time with new ideas. Asa had a new idea, too, and filed a patent for it in October of 1924. The patent read, in part:

"Certain commodities, such as flour, are put in sacks of textile material and such sacks are provided with characters designating the trade mark or brand and the manufacturer, jobber, or dealer. Such sacks, however, usually serve no useful purpose, except that of holding the product for shipment or until used.

One of the objects of this invention is to provide a package having a sack, the cloth of which is adapted to be used for dress goods after the product has been removed or consumed."

The application went on to detail the sack should be "of a size suitable of being remade into clothing" and "with a substantially indelible or permanent pattern." The preferable pattern would be cotton gingham "having stripes or checks in two or more colors." Markings such as the company name should be of ink that would wash away so the cloth could be used for making dresses or other clothing items.

Asa Bales assigned the patent to George P. Plant Milling Company of St. Louis, Missouri, who moved quickly to put the pretty sacks in the hands of the consumer. Gingham Girl, in a variety of colors and featuring a charming southern belle, was

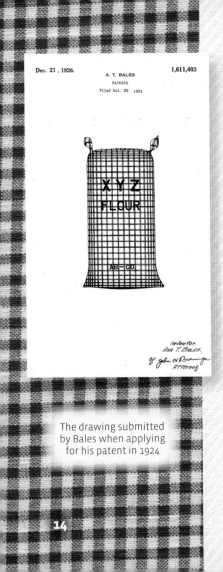

Dec. 21, 1926.
A. T. BALES
PACKAGE
Filed Oct. 29, 1924
1,611,403

X Y Z
FLOUR

ABC CO.

Inventor.
Asa T. Bales.
By John N. Browning
Attorney.

The drawing submitted by Bales when applying for his patent in 1924

introduced through the pages of *The Northwestern Miller* on April 15, 1925, in this announcement:

Gingham Is Used for Flour Sacks: George P. Plant Milling Co., St. Louis, Employs a Novel Idea in Marketing New Flour

In an attempt to get away from the customary methods of merchandising flour, wherein quality, ash and protein content, service, co-operation and like points are the principle selling arguments advanced by the great majority of mill representatives, the George P. Plant Milling Co., St. Louis, has introduced on the market flour packed in gingham sacks, and registered under the Gingham trademark.

To bring out the individuality of the flour in such a way that the housewife will immediately recognize the outstanding characteristics of that flour and demand it is difficult, not only because of the similarity in the quality of flours, but also because of the frequent sameness in flour packages. In explaining the reasons for the adoption of gingham cloth for flour sacks and the accompanying Gingham trademark, E. L. Stancliff, general manager of the company, said:

"We have tried to get away from the old commonplace method of selling flour. The great mistake we millers have made in the

past has been the general custom of discussing flour grades and flour markets with the dealer instead of placing our entire emphasis upon developing a kind of flour and a merchandising plan that will assure the dealer a profit.

"We have all been guilty of selling just flour by grades, comparing one flour with another and getting the flour merchant's mind centered on a kind of flour instead of upon new ideas that will make money for him."

The trademark for the new sack is Gingham, under which come a number of different brands, of which the principal one is Gingham Girl. Others are Mother Gingham, Baby Gingham and Gingham Queen. These brands, and others, have already gained a wide distribution and are well established in several markets.

Before starting the merchandising of Gingham brands the Plant company saw to it that its trademark was protected in every way. The use of gingham for flour bags is protected by registrations, patents and copyrights, which are the sole property of the George P. Plant Milling Co. The company has also secured the only other registration covering gingham for a food package ever made, and the only other flour mill that has ever used gingham sacks has recognized Plant's prior and exclusive rights, withdrawn its brands from the market and assigned its business, on gingham packed flour, to the Plant company.

15

GINGHAM IS USED
FOR FLOUR SACKS

George P. Plant Milling Co., St. Louis, Employs a Novel Idea in Marketing New Flour

St. Louis, Mo.—In an attempt to get away from the customary methods of merchandising flour, wherein quality, ash and protein content, service, co-operation and like points are the principle selling arguments advanced by the great majority of mill representatives, the George P. Plant Milling Co., St. Louis, has introduced on the market flour packed in gingham sacks, and registered under the Gingham trademark.

To bring out the individuality of a flour in such a way that the housewife will immediately recognize the outstanding characteristics of that flour and demand it is difficult, not only because of the similarity in the quality of flours, but also because of the frequent sameness in flour packages. In explaining the reasons for the adoption of gingham cloth for flour sacks and the accompanying Gingham trademark, E. L. Stancliff, general manager of the company, said:

"We have tried to get away from the old commonplace method of selling flour. The great mistake we millers have made in the past has been the general custom of discussing flour grades and flour markets with the dealer instead of placing our entire emphasis upon developing a kind of flour and a merchandising plan that will assure the dealer a profit.

"We have all been guilty of selling just flour by grades, comparing one flour with another and getting the flour merchant's mind centered on a kind of flour instead of upon new ideas that will make money for him."

The trademark for the new sack is Gingham, under which come a number of different brands, of which the principal one is Gingham Girl. Others are Mother Gingham, Baby Gingham and Gingham Queen. These brands, and others, have already gained a wide distribution and are well established in several markets.

Before starting the merchandising of Gingham brands the Plant company saw to it that its trademark was protected in every way. The use of gingham for flour bags is protected by registrations, patents and copyrights, which are the sole property of the George P. Plant Milling Co. The company has also se-

cured the only other registration covering gingham for a food package ever made, and the only other flour mill that has ever used gingham sacks has recognized Plant's prior and exclusive rights, withdrawn its brands from the market and assigned its business, on gingham packed flour, to the Plant company.

Bread, pastry and fancy cake flours are being packed under the Gingham brands. The gingham used in the sacks, is a

plain piece of gingham, its size dependent upon the size of the flour sack purchased, a circumstance that appeals strongly to the housewife, for the gingham thus obtained can be used for making dresses, aprons, rompers and a number of other useful articles.

"The distinctive feature of the Gingham brand," Mr. Stancliff explained, "appeals to the dealer and jobber alike, because it is packed in a bag that cannot be imitated. Gingham Girl is a different kind of flour, and in placing it on the market we have endeavored to develop

a plan that will enable the flour merchant to make a profit on every barrel of flour he sells, by removing him from price competition."

In co-operating with its distributors the milling company is using many forms of merchandising tie-ups, all looking toward the end of placing the flour in the hands of the ultimate consumers. The individuality of the Gingham trademark is unique, and the brands are meeting with marked success.

W. G. MARTIN, JR.

CONTINENTAL'S PURCHASE OF
CANADIAN MILL DENIED

Montreal, Que.—A rumor that the Continental Baking Corporation has been negotiating for purchase of the St. Lawrence Flour Mills, Muncy, Pa., in connection with its Canadian plans, is officially denied in both Montreal and New York.

A. H. BAILEY.

PENNSYLVANIA INSTITUTIONS
TO TEST NEW FLOUR BLEND

Pittsburgh, Pa.—In order that state institutions may obtain their bread at a lower cost, the use of a blend of flour milled in Pennsylvania containing 50 per cent of wheat grown in that state and 50 per cent spring wheat is to be tried. A series of baking demonstrations has been planned as a result of one recently held at the Allentown State Hospital.

George A. Stuart, Pennsylvania bureau of markets, with the assistance of W. G. Goodenow, chemist at the City Flouring Mills, Muncy, Pa., a demonstrator, New York City, and Walter Marshall, United States Department of Agriculture, will be responsible for the demonstrations.

The institutions which are arranging for the demonstrations are anxious to secure this information, since bread is one of the most important items on their daily menu. They include the Eastern State Penitentiary, Philadelphia; the

and distributed among the various co-operatives and bakers, which measure is supposed to relieve the situation somewhat. In order to improve the position of the unemployed, various reconstruction plans are being considered by the government. One of them calls for the reconstruction of Petrograd, involving the expenditure of 30,850,000 rubles. The plan has been confirmed by the council of labor and defense, and must be realized within the period of five years. It is reported that the Gostorg has shipped a trial consignment of Russian alcoholic beverages to Sweden with a view to introduce this product on the Swedish market, according to Commercial Attaché Mayer, at Riga, Latvia.

FIRST STEAMER OF SEASON
ARRIVES IN DULUTH HARBOR

Duluth, Minn.—The steamer Harvester reached Duluth at 11:45 a.m., April 14, from Chicago, the first arrival of the season. She started without cargo from Chicago, and intends to load ore at Duluth.

The navigation season will not be officially opened in the grain trade until May 1, but another boat is reported to have arrived from Lake Erie and is now loading wheat from the elevators.

The steamer Robbins, scheduled to leave Duluth for Buffalo April 13, ran aground in the harbor, and tugs failed to release her. Her departure is now indefinitely delayed.

F. G. CARLSON.

SUPPLEMENTAL TARIFFS ON
GRAIN EXPORTS SUSPENDED

Seattle, Wash.—The Interstate Commerce Commission has suspended, until Aug. 21, supplemental tariffs filed by the Northern Pacific, Great Northern and Milwaukee railroads, canceling the export rate on Montana grain and grain products shipped through north Pacific Coast ports. The export rate has been 7c cwt less than the domestic rate. The suspension of the tariffs was granted in order to give hearings to protests made by Montana wheat farmers and north Pacific Coast millers and grain dealers against the canceling of the export rate.

A Commission examiner, who recently heard testimony in regard to the export rate, reported that he considered the rates fully justified and advised the Commission to uphold them. Just before final argument before the Commission the railroads ordered the rates canceled, effective April 23.

In their petition against the suspension of the export rate the coast interests laid stress on the necessity of rates which would permit the hard wheat growers of Montana to meet the competition of Canadian hard wheat in the oriental flour and grain trade. Since the export rate was placed in force, export rates from Canadian provinces to Vancouver, B. C., have been reduced 10 per cent and are now 25 to 30 per cent less than those of the American railroads.

PITTSBURGH FLOUR CLUB
HELD MEETING APRIL 11

Pittsburgh, Pa.—The Pittsburgh Flour Club met at the Fort Pitt Hotel on April 11, when I. E. Bowman, vice president, presided in the absence of Harlow S. Lewis, who was unable to attend.

A warm welcome was given to Jesse C. Stewart, of the Stewart C. Stewart Co., by the members in honor of his return from South America. A. P. Cole and Harlow S. Lewis were elected as delegates to the annual convention of the National Federated Flour Clubs to be held in Baltimore in June.

PROGRAM IS ANNOUNCED
FOR FEDERATION MEETING

Chicago, Ill.—The annual convention of the Millers' National Federation at Edgewater Beach Hotel, will be called to order by T. S. Blish, chairman of the board at 10 a.m., April 16 when reports of officers, standing committees and the executive committee will be heard. At the afternoon session, B. W. Marr will be installed as the new chairman of the board.

Following remarks by Mr. Marr there will be discussion of a report by the executive committee. Recommendations of this committee will be presented by Sydney Anderson, president of the Federation. Other matters to receive attention at this time are the adoption of a code of ethics and business practices, and the appointment of a controllers council. Discussion of the latter question will be led by Charles R. Stevenson Stevenson Corporation, New York City.

Revision of the articles of organization will be proposed in the report of a standing committee, and action called for. The last business of this session will be the proposed revision of the Millers' National Federation uniform sales contract. Discussion will be led by Carl W. Sims, of the committee on sales contract.

On the evening of April 16 a dinner will be given at Edgewater Beach with Curtis M. Johnson as speaker.

At the Friday morning session there will be a report from the nominating committee on election of directors, and an address by Thad L. Hoffman, president Kansas Flour Mills Co., on "Profit: Excess of Income Over Expenditure." At the afternoon session there is scheduled a full discussion of subjects of general interest, such as confidence, the fallacy of selling flour for distant future shipment, replacement value as the proper basis for wheat in figuring the cost of flour. The new board of directors will meet to elect two vice chairmen, the executive committee, president, secretary-treasurer and other officers. Directors whose terms expire are Henry M. Allen, H. L. Beecher, W. L. Harvey, H. S. Helm, E. M. Kelly, F. T. King, A. C. Loring, B. W. Marr, Thomas L. Moore, Guy A. Thomas, and George P. Urban.

A. P. Husband, secretary, is sending out a program for the meeting with a bulletin asking for a large attendance of millers, so that plans for the coming year's activities can be carried out to the fullest extent. He points out that these plans, to be effective, must have the earnest support of every miller. Officers of the Federation look to this meeting for definite instructions.

Golfers are notified that arrangements will be made at the hotel to play on one of the courses lying within a short distance of the meeting place. Officers, however, do not want golf to interfere with attendance.

SOUTHERN MILLS ARE
DESTROYED BY FIRE

Nashville, Tenn.—Fire of undetermined origin completely ruined the plant of the Oneida (Tenn.) Milling Co., early last week, causing a loss estimated at $80,000. The plant was built of brick and concrete about five years ago, and was one of the most modern in the Oneida section. Considerable grain and other stock were destroyed. The loss was partly covered by insurance.

CALIFORNIA WRAPPED BREAD
BILL WITHDRAWN BY SPONSOR

Los Angeles, Cal.—The Senate bread

laundry soap and water. This leaves a plain piece of gingham, its size dependent upon the size of the flour sack purchased, a circumstance that appeals strongly to the housewife, for the gingham thus obtained can be used for making dresses, aprons, rompers and a number of other useful articles.

"The distinctive feature of the Gingham brand," Mr. Stancliff explained, "appeals to the dealer and jobber alike because it is packed in a bag that cannot be imitated. Gingham Girl is a different kind of flour, and in placing it on the market we have endeavored to develop a plan that will enable the flour merchant to make a profit on every barrel of flour he sells, by removing him from price competition."

In co-operating with its distributors the milling company is using many forms of merchandising tie-ups, all looking toward the end of placing the flour in the hands of the ultimate consumers. The individuality of the Gingham trademark is unique, and the brands are meeting with marked success.

W. G. Martin, Jr.

The first advertisements for the new Gingham Girl dress goods sack appeared in June of 1925 in *The Northwestern Miller*:

The response to our announcement of Gingham Girl Flour, packed only in bags of real high grade gingham, has been spontaneous and wide-spread. Distributors have been quick to realize the remarkable merchandising advantages of this distinctive brand. If you have not already done so, write or wire at once for available territory. It will mean real profit to you to handle GINGHAM GIRL— 'the world's finest flour'. – Geo. P. Plant Milling Co.

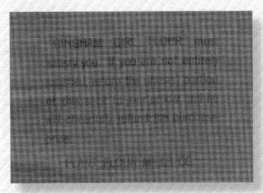

A ten pound sack of Gingham Girl Flour in the early pink and white gingham. The checks are very small at only one-sixth inch.

The back of the sack carried this guarantee, "Gingham Girl Flour must satisfy you. If you are not entirely satisfied, return the unused portion of this sack to your grocer and he will cheerfully refund the purchase price. – Plant Flour Mills Co."

1925 and Beyond

What happened to Asa? Sadly, little more is known about his life. The last records uncovered are from April of 1927, and find him moving to Salina, Kansas, to take the position of Sales Manager at Weber Flour Mills. Within days of his arrival, the area was inundated by floodwaters, with scant milling news for months. No trace of him has been found in a later census, social security records, military records or the like. As for his wife and son, Allene remarried in 1927 and Robert remained with her.

We do know what happened to Asa's invention. The George P. Plant Milling Company continued to promote gingham dress print bags through the use of clever advertising and giveaways. One was a handy, pocket-sized notebook for the customer's record keeping needs. Another was a booth display of Gingham Girl Flour at the annual convention of the Associated Bakers of America, held in St. Louis in May of 1926. An unusual advertising method was the appearance of a live Gingham Girl during the 1927 Convention of the American Wholesale Grocers' Association in Louisville, Kentucky. (photo on page 21.)

SALINA

There was a little more life to flour business here last week, and shipping directions were a little more free. Prices are unchanged from last week. Quotations, March 31, basis Kansas City, cotton 98's: short patent, $7.10@7.50 bbl; 95 per cent, $6.80@7; straight, $6.70@ 6.80.

NOTES

Continued rains brighten the already optimistic outlook for the new wheat crop in this section, which is better than for seven or eight years.

A. T. Bales and family arrived here last week from St. Louis by motor. Mr. Bales took up his work as sales manager of the Weber Flour Mills Co. on April 1.

The Northwestern Miller, April 6, 1927, announced A. T. Bales arrived for his new position in Salina, Kansas.

Gingham Girl Pocket
Notebook from 1925.
Front and Back Covers.

20

Inside pages

A View Showing the Majority of the Booths at the Bakery Exhibition in the New Coliseum, St. Louis, May 3-8; Model Bakery in the Background

Gingham Girl Flour in dress print bags was displayed in "an attractively decorated
booth" at the 1926 convention of the Associated Bakers of America in St. Louis.
The American Baker, May 26, 1926*
*All photos, articles, advertisements, etc. from *The American Baker* are reprinted courtesy of The Miller Publishing Company

Representatives of the Plant Flour Mills Co. at the Recent Convention of the American Wholesale Grocers' Association in Louisville, Ky. Left to Right, E. L. Stancliff, general manager; the "Gingham Girl"; John M. Burch; J. G. Schmitz.

The Gingham Girl makes an appearance at the 1927 Convention of the American Wholesale Grocers' Association. *The Northwestern Miller*, June 1, 1927

Gingham Feedsacks

Woven dress gingham in checks, stripes and plaids was the fabric of choice for the first dress print bags. It was more popular than calico, held up well to laundering, was colorfast and had a fresh, light look. Calico had fallen out of favor due to inferior quality and the frequent use of dark colors. It faded and did not stand up to wear. Gingham was the better value and for a few more years, the one desired by the customer.

The following are examples of dress gingham yard goods available by mail order during the time period of Asa Bales' invention. Two to four colors were common in woven dress gingham from this decade.

Gingham is advertised on the front cover of the Summer 1923 Montgomery Ward & Co. Sale Catalog. Some of the featured color combinations were green and tangerine; pink and green; lavender and green; red and navy blue; tan and blue. Pages used with permission of Midwest Catalog Brands, Inc. Montgomery Ward and Wards are registered marks of Midwest Catalog Brands, Inc.

More gingham from the Summer 1923 Montgomery Ward & Co. Sale Catalog. Pages used with permission of Midwest Catalog Brands, Inc. Montgomery Ward and Wards are registered marks of Midwest Catalog Brands, Inc.

Our Leader 32 in. Dress Gingham

18¢
A Yard

Width, about 32 inches

Gingham always is a favored fabric for women's and children's wash dresses. It is nice for dresses. It is nice for neat allover aprons, and makes very pretty and inexpensive draperies for kitchen, nursery or sewing room windows.

Attractively Priced

This quality is firmly woven of good cotton yarns. It is easily washed and ironed. Our price for this desirable quality is very low. You will make a worthwhile saving by ordering now. Consider the wearing quality and you will appreciate the value of this material.

PATTERNS AND COLORS: As illustrated.

State pattern number wanted.

16 C 3128—Per yard........18¢
Postage, per yard, 1¢ extra

Lingette
Everybody Thinks it's Silk

59¢
A Yard

Width, about 36 inches

Garments made of Lingette may be washed time and again, ironed on the right side, and never lose their luster. Made of extra strength, long fiber cotton, fine spun with the long wearing and excellent laundering qualities that you get only in fine cotton. The permanent stripe is woven into the material. Looks like an all silk fabric with its pleasing permanent mercerized finish. There is only one grade of genuine Lingette, and you get that grade from Ward's. The name Lingette is on the selvedge of every piece. Used for women's undergarments, bloomers and shadow-proof slips; children's clothes; men's shirts and pajamas; comforter coverings; hat, coat and cape linings.

COLORS: White; flesh; peach; shirting (light) blue; orchid; tan; navy blue; Kelly green; medium brown; light gray; Copenhagen blue; rose; purple; or black. State color wanted.

16 C 3042—Per yard..59¢
Postage, per yard, 1¢ extra

Novelty Percale

17¢
A Yard

Width, about 36 inches

These Novelty Percale Prints are proving very popular for women's afternoon and morning dresses, children's school and play clothes; in fact, there are patterns and colors suitable for garments for everyone in the family. Some of the patterns are also pretty for draperies.

Well woven of good cotton yarns. These patterns, copied from the favored English prints, are woven and printed in America. Attractive and durable cloth for such a low price.

PATTERNS AND COLORS: As illustrated.
State pattern number wanted.

16 C 3205—Per yard..........17¢
Postage, per yard, 1¢ extra

The Oldest Mail Order House Is Today the Most Progressive

$1.39
A Bundle

Lengths from

Width, about

Many yards of remnants are put up in these bundles. will make a substantial materials. Can be used everyday garments and the house.

This bundle is made up of ten y Percales in useful lengths from 1 have found that they can make a lengths this way. We do not ma

16 C 936—Per bundle.........
Postage, per bund

Fast Color Dress Gingham

28¢
A Yard

Width, about 32 inc

Guaranteed fast color Gingham in designs. Woven of long staple cotton yarn —one of the best dyeing processes known and still hold their dainty color. For spr

PATTERNS AND COLORS: (1) Even c tangerine, light blue or black. (2) Go plaid. (3) Copenhagen blue, gold and (4) Tan with crossbar of Copenhagen or tangerine with crossbar of helio. (5) Copenhagen blue or helio with bla effect. (6) Rose with green, gold an helio with white. (7) Novelty checks of pink, Copenhagen and black plaid. (8) Copenhagen blu

State pattern number and colo

16 C 3173—Per yard..........
Postage, per yard, 1¢ ex

24

The 1930s brought changes in the dress print bag* with the appearance of pastels and calicoes. These changes will be examined in detail in the following chapter.

Dress print bag is the term used in early advertisements for patterned flour and feed sacks. Today the most common usage is feedsack and includes all the various sacks or bags used to hold human and animal food such as flour, meal, sugar, salt, farm feeds, etc. Some non-food products, such as fertilizer, were also packaged in dress print bags.

740

- INK EASILY REMOVED -
Don't Soak, but scrub thoroly
with warm water and soap.

"My mamma made all these things from
COTTON BAGS

GINGHAM GIRL

The
World's
Finest
Flour

The
Gingham Girl

Made by Millers of
WHITE STAR
The Baker's Flour   Dependable Since 1840
Plant Flour Mills Company
ST. LOUIS, MO., U. S. A.

— Chapter Two. —
The 1930s: Gingham, Pastel & Calico

The Great Depression coupled with the Dust Bowl brought hardship to a nation. As the drought spread to more than seventy-five percent of the country, news in the milling periodicals took on a somber tone. Cropland and livestock were lost at an alarming rate. Many families had no choice but to leave their homes and farms behind and start anew. Others who stayed on the land tried to find a little humor in the situation and said they were "trading" farms as precious topsoil blew from one state to another.

In the early summer of 1934, the federal government created a Drought Relief Service to purchase starving cattle from areas designated as emergencies. Any not fit for use in human food or too weak to survive the train trip to the packinghouse were immediately destroyed and buried. The rest were used in food relief programs. Payments were based on a number of factors, including condition of the animal, its weight and the region of the country. Calves could bring as little as $4 to $5 in some states or as much as $8 in others. Benefit payments for yearlings ranged from $10 to $15. Payments were slightly higher for cows, at $12 to $20. According to Donald Worster in *Dust Bowl: The Southern Plains in the 1930's*, the program met with resistance at the start, but as the weeks progressed and the drought intensified, farmers finally gave in to the DSR. Many were already on the brink of financial ruin and realized the government was offering fair compensation for starving animals. When the program ended in 1935, 8.3 million head of cattle had been purchased for a grand total of $111.7 million. For the first

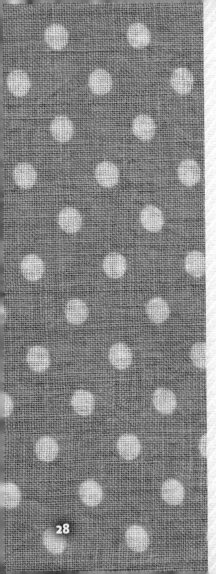

time, the U.S. government owned more cattle than anyone in the world.

The poultry industry also suffered mightily. The *Oklahoma Historical Society's Encyclopedia of Oklahoma History & Culture* explains in 1927, an Oklahoma chicken had a value of eighty cents. By 1934 the figure was a mere twenty-seven cents. From 1927 to 1935, the state's chicken population decreased by over five million. As profits tumbled, many farmers gave up on the poultry business.

A sharp dive in both the production and consumption of food products, including flour, occurred nationwide. In 1929 the U.S. consumer spent a total of $19.5 billion on food. Four years later and with a growing population, the number was markedly lower at only $11.6 billion. The prosperity of the Roaring Twenties was but a memory, as many no longer had the means to purchase nourishment for the day.

Franklin D. Roosevelt, elected for a second term, addressed an anxious people on January 20, 1937. The following is a portion from his inaugural address:

> *I see millions of families trying to live on incomes so meager that the pall of family disaster hangs over them day by day.*

> *I see millions whose daily lives in city and on farm continue under conditions labeled indecent by a so-called polite society half a century ago.*

> *I see millions denied education, recreation, and the opportunity*

to better their lot and the lot of their children.

I see millions lacking the means to buy the products of farm and factory and by their poverty denying work and productiveness to many other millions.

I see one-third of a nation ill-housed, ill-clad, ill-nourished.

It is not in despair that I paint you that picture. I paint it for you in hope--because the Nation, seeing and understanding the injustice in it, proposes to paint it out. We are determined to make every American citizen the subject of his country's interest and concern; and we will never regard any faithful law-abiding group within our borders as superfluous. The test of our progress is not whether we add more to the abundance of those who have much; it is whether we provide enough for those who have too little.

Under Roosevelt's leadership, Congress passed various relief and reform measures with the goal of making the economy secure, improving social welfare and preventing future depressions. Slowly, the country began to emerge from the darkest days of the Great Depression. In view of the economic circumstances, it is amazing to find any mention of dress print bags during this time, but there are some. The following were found in the archives:

Two references to gingham bags are noted in milling periodicals from 1932. One is a short article and the other an advertisement.

FLOUR MILL USES GINGHAM

DALLAS, TEXAS.—The Dittlinger Roller Mills of New Braunfels in the future will use gingham manufactured by the New Braunfels Textile Mills in sacking its flour. The management of the mills says the flour sacks will be of the conventional small and large check gingham and the printing on the sack will be of ink which can be washed off easily with warm water. The gingham used for flour sacks will be guaranteed fast colors. Hence the housewife when buying a sack of flour will also be getting a yard of 32-inch gingham.

"Flour Mill Uses Gingham" Dittlinger Roller Mills to use small and large check gingham. "The gingham used for the flour sacks will be guaranteed fast colors. Hence the housewife when buying a sack of flour will also be getting a yard of 32-inch gingham." Feedstuffs, June 11, 1932*
*All photos, articles, advertisements, etc. from Feedstuffs are reprinted courtesy of The Miller Publishing Company

It was in 1936, with government programs underway and unemployment improving from 24.9 to 17.0 percent, that advertising for dress print bags resumed. A full-page advertisement for Gingham Girl Flour in "assorted colors and designs, with a strong appeal to every housewife buyer" ran in the July 15, 1936, *Northwestern Miller*. Ads continued through the year and into the next with each one taking a different sales approach.

Ad for Gingham Girl "The World's Finest Flour"
The Northwestern Miller and
American Baker, January 6, 1932

"Assorted colors
and designs"
*The Northwestern
Miller*, July 15, 1936

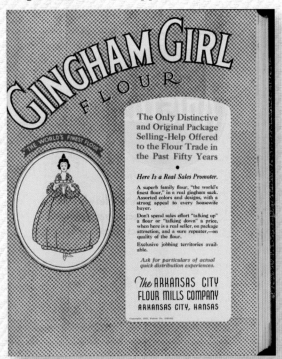

Gingham Girl Flour Sack
Note the "enriched" stamping which dates this sack
to no earlier than 1938, when flour enrichment in
the United States began on a limited scale.

Close up of Gingham Girl Flour Sack in a deep pink-red and white.

Pastels in the 1930s

In 1936, the Arkansas City Flour Mills introduced something new to their customers: flour "packed in fast-color sacks (nine assorted pastel shades) of excellent fabric, for which every housewife can find a hundred uses." The sacks were available in pink, lavender, orchid, tea rose, peach, yellow, rose, blue and tan. Richard Peek, then vice-president of the Percy Kent Bag Company of Kansas City, Missouri, is credited with the idea for the pastel sacks. According to the company booklet, *PK: Our First Hundred Years*, Mr. Peek was having breakfast in a Wichita, Kansas hotel when "he noticed that the backs of the wooden chairs had removable cotton slip covers of various pastel shades. Yellow, pink, green and light blue and violet. Why, he thought, wouldn't bags made out of these shades be a knockout with the housewife? Would they indeed!" His idea was successful and helped make Percy Kent a leader in the cotton bag industry.

Pastel Feedsacks

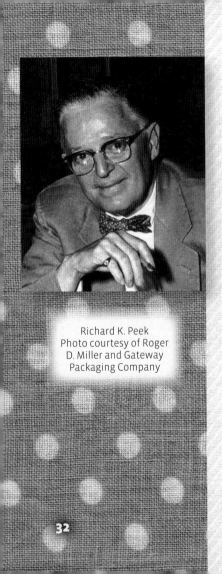

Richard K. Peek
Photo courtesy of Roger D. Miller and Gateway Packaging Company

Pastell and Pastel Girl brand flours from the Arkansas City Flour Mills Company of Arkansas City, Kansas, could be purchased in the new, softly colored cotton bags from the Percy Kent Bag Company.

In 1937, the Arkansas City Flour Mills Company advertised a triple bonus sack -- pastel, needlework and apron all in one. It was designed and made by Percy Kent.

Pastell Flour in nine shades of "beautiful fast color fabric"
The Northwestern Miller, June 24, 1936

(far left) Pastel Girl Flour "packed in fast color sacks... for which every housewife can find a hundred uses."
The Northwestern Miller, June 29, 1936

(left) "Now You Can Junk Your Old Used Sacks" *The Northwestern Miller* and *American Baker*, June 2, 1937

This Tint-sax held 100 lbs. of Critic Feeds from Schultz, Baujan & Co.

Tint-sax (later known as Kentex) was the name used by the Percy Kent Bag Co. for their line of pastel sacks. Even after several washings, the logo is still visible on many sacks. Instructions for removing ink are, "Don't soak, but scrub thoroly (sic) with warm water and soap."

Staley Milling advertised their products were available in ten different "Tint-sax" pastels. *Feedstuffs*, March 13, 1937

Calico and Novelty Dress Print Bags Appear

We've looked at advertising for gingham and pastel but what about the calico sack? It was the end of the 1930s before calico feed sacks appeared in milling advertisements. That's not to say they weren't already in use. Is there any evidence, then, that calico dress bags existed in the 1930s? Yes, there is.

The Bemis Company website, www.bemis150.com, explains they began to sell the decorative, patterned feed and flour sacks "during the 1930s." These fancy prints could be used in sewing many household items from quilts and draperies to dresses and children's clothing.

Margaret Bourke-White from *Life* magazine, who received nationwide acclaim for her photographs of individuals and families in the drought-and-depression weary south, snapped two interesting flour sack photographs in 1939. They can be viewed in the online Life Photo Archives at http://images.google.com/hosted/life.* (It will help to type "printed flour sacks" in the website's search bar.) The photos were taken at the Sunbonnet Sue Flour Mill in Wichita, Kansas, and picture twenty-four and ninety-eight pound bags of flour in a surprising range of prints from the typical calico to several novelty dress prints. One sack has small-scale dancers in billowy skirts; another is a curtain or tablecloth print. Look closely in the background of the photo with the Rabbit toy backprint and you will see the following Hansel and Gretel flour sack:

Editor's note: Please keep in mind that web sites are subject to change and sometimes disappear completely.

Hansel and Gretel Novelty Flour Sack, available by 1939. Notice the use of four colors: medium blue, navy, red and salmon-pink.

A second colorway was available in red, blue, green and yellow.

The Hansel and Gretel print was also available in convenient six and twelve pound sizes. The labels have the "PK" logo of the Percy Kent Bag Company.

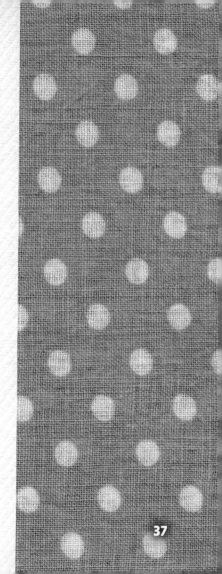

Calico feedsacks were used in Oklahoma during the depression. In 1942 Gertrude Allen Dinsmore, from the *Los Angeles Times,* traveled to Farmer's Hill, in rural McCurtain County, to observe the use of colorful sack prints in an area where every penny mattered. What she found was surprising. Nearly everyone in the county was proud to wear "feed-bag" clothing. She was told that during the depression, an Oklahoma miller listened to so many complaints about garments made from the scratchy, uncomfortable feedsacks with inked advertising that wouldn't launder out, he decided to do something about it. He contacted Pacific Mills who agreed to design attractive bag prints in a better quality, soft cloth. These bags were stamped with wash away labels so, at long last, rural school children could wear stylish clothing made from feed-bag material. Customers were thrilled and demand grew for the pretty cloth. Ms. Dinsmore reported the most popular patterns were children's novelties and those with designs in squares, since they worked well in quilting. So eager were the women to get enough sacks of a certain pattern for a dress, quilt or home project, they held "bag parties" to trade sacks. By early 1942, bright, new prints arrived almost weekly in the local J. S. Miller's store and added only five cents to the cost of the grain or feed.

In *Texas Quilts and Quilters: A Lone Star Legacy*, author Marcia Kaylakie shares a novelty flour sack that played a part in Texas history. It is important in feedsack history, too, with evidence of being the earliest novelty dress print sack found thus far. Its cloth tells a story of Texas music, radio, politics and Hillbilly Flour from the W. Lee O'Daniel Flour Company of Ft. Worth, Texas. The company was founded in 1935 by Wilbert Lee "Pappy" O'Daniel who gathered a western swing band called the Hillbilly Boys and booked them on WBAP radio to promote his flour. The daily

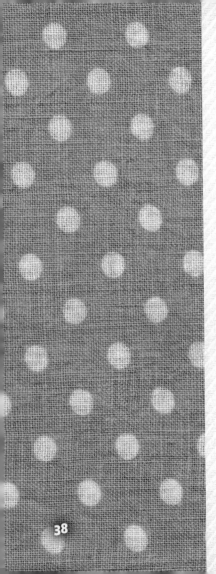

program opened with *"Please pass the biscuits, Pappy"* followed by fifteen minutes of Texas swing and Pappy's talk. Catchy jingles filled the airwaves. *"Hillbilly music on the air, Hillbilly Flour everywhere. It tickles your feet - It tickles your tongue, Wherever you go - Its praises are sung!"* Listeners were drawn to Pappy's old-fashioned, relaxed style and sales of his flour increased. Not to be overlooked in the success are the sacks that held O'Daniel Flour. One was made to reuse as a toy. It had a billy goat on the front and a band member doll on the back. Another was a brightly colored dress print with pictures of the Hillbilly Boys, band instruments, song titles and Texas symbols. To help narrow a time frame when this novelty dress print sack appeared, let's see what happened next in the Hillbilly Flour story.

By the spring of 1938, Pappy's interests turned to politics, with the surprising announcement he planned to run for Governor. The Hillbilly Boys and O'Daniel's flour were included and became crucial to his election strategy. At each stop along the campaign trail, the Hillbilly Boys worked the crowds with music, then Pappy led the band in singing their most requested "Beautiful Texas," a hit song they recorded with the Vocalion record label the previous year. Next he talked on the importance of following the Golden Rule and Ten Commandments. When the crowd was sufficiently wooed with music, the Bible and political promises, he sent his teenagers, Pat, Mike and Molly, into the audience to pass small donation barrels labeled "Flour Not Pork." The entertainment approach to politics paid off handsomely in flour sales. O'Daniel, a salesman at heart, was heard to say, "I don't know whether or not I'll get elected, but, boy! it sure is good for the flour business."[1]

[1]*Time, "Flour Salesman," July 25, 1938*

On January 17, 1939, Wilbert Lee O'Daniel became the thirty-fourth Governor of Texas. For a few weeks, he savored the victory and enjoyed his new status in both politics and business. It soon became evident his political knowledge was lacking which led to conflicts with the legislature. O'Daniel had earlier made the campaign pledge to block any sales tax and give old-age pensions of $30 a month for those over sixty-five years of age. In reality he did the opposite and tried to gather support for a 1.6 percent transaction tax in order to finance the pension plan. This move infuriated many, including grocers who refused to sell Hillbilly Flour. To make matters worse, a tithe certificate was enclosed in the sacks of flour that year. The consumer could donate it to his church, which would then have a share in the O'Daniel Company. With grocers shunning the flour, sales plunged and profits disappeared. Pappy's sons sent letters to all certificate-holding pastors, explaining there were no funds to divide. O'Daniel, aware of the effect it could have on his career, tithed ten percent of his salary for the year and divided it among them. The payments varied from as little as five cents to $24, with an average of only $1.43.[2]

During this same time, tension escalated between O'Daniel and his Hillbilly Boys over a pay raise. Two band members left the group before O'Daniel's second run for Governor in 1940. One was steel guitarist Kermit Whalen; the other was vocalist Leon Huff. Both are pictured on the novelty flour sack as "Happy Horace" and "Leon the Texas Song Bird." With the original band no longer together and popularity of Hillbilly Flour diminishing, it seems logical to give a pre-1939 date to the novelty "Beautiful Texas" flour sack. Emphasis can be placed on 1938 when O'Daniel and the Hillbilly Boys toured in the sound-equipped vehicle, played "Beautiful Texas" to mark the opening of each political rally and were recognized

[2]*Time, "O'Daniel Pays His Tithe," April 29, 1940*

in both radio and politics by the slogan, "Please Pass the Biscuits, Pappy."

Additional evidence for dating this print can be found in photographs from the *Official Souvenir Program* for the 9th Annual Prison Rodeo held in Huntsville, Texas, in 1939. In one, O'Daniel and his Hillbilly Band perform in shirts made from the "Beautiful Texas" novelty sack fabric. In another, W. Lee O'Daniel sits in the grandstand, shirt clearly visible. Both photos are dated, "last year's rodeo," placing the novelty flour sack fabric in use by 1938.

Dress Print Bags in Interviews and Advertising

Governor O'Daniel and His Famous Hillbilly Band at Last Year's Rodeo

A photo from the *1939 Official Souvenir Program* for the 9th Annual Prison Rodeo, Huntsville, Texas. Notice the print on the shirts. The page heading is "Governor O'Daniel and His Famous Hillbilly Band at Last Year's Rodeo." Photo courtesy of the Texas Department of Criminal Justice, Huntsville.

Interviews are a valuable source of information on early feedsack prints. Ruth Rhoades, author of *Feed Sacks in Georgia*, conducted well over two hundred interviews to analyze "the manufacture, marketing, and use of feed sacks in Georgia." The data provided "forty-three references which document the existence of feed-sack prints between 1927 and 1937." It is noteworthy that a number of the participants were able to connect an important event, such as the birth of a child or a start of a new job, with the existence of feedsack prints and thus establish a date and location for them.

Advertisements in milling periodicals for calico dress print bags began as the 1930s drew to a close. In an August 1939 ad, Kasco Bags were said to be "the best merchandising idea brought into the feed business in a coon's age" and available "in a host of different colors and patterns." The fine print along the bottom of the ad explained Kasco Feeds were "sold only in territory east of the Ohio-Indiana state line." As previously noted, patterned and novelty sacks were available in other areas of the country before this date.

The Werthan-Morgan-Hamilton Bag Company was a leader in using quality cotton in their bags. According to the company's website, http://www.werthan.com/wpihistory.htm, Werthan made "higher quality 'dress print' bags" in the late 1930s.

Werthan and other bag companies advertised on sewing items. This "Sew Easy with Werthan Bags" needle book reminded the user to, "Ask that your flour, meal, feed and fertilizer be packed in Werthco dress print bags and have the best!"

Kasco advertised their bags had "Sax Appeal." Their "Dress Print Sax" logo is stamped in the upper left corner of this 100 lb. sack of feed.

Feedsack Backprints

The Thirties would not be complete without mention of the fun backprints, also known as needlework imprints, that were printed on the back side of the sacks. Backprints included toys, aprons, doilies, collar and cuff sets, tea towels and other items. The Percy Kent Bag Company was the leader in this style of sack. Following are some advertisements for them:

Humpty Dumpty, Rabbit and Camel Toys were popular backprints for the youngsters.
The Northwestern Miller, March 31, 1937

(far right) Percy Kent's Needlework Sak with Washout Inks
All-Week Tea Towels with embroidered Sunbonnet Lady
The Northwestern Miller, April 14, 1937

(near right) Needlework for bridge table doilies
could be found on some Percy Kent "PK" bags.
The Northwestern Miller, May 12, 1937

(below) Apron with stamped embroidery
for the Three Little Pigs
One of many ads with reasons why "Mr. Miller"
should package his product in PK backprint bags.
The Northwestern Miller and *American Baker*, May 4, 1938

This 24 lb. cambric flour sack has a "Mexicana" tea towel backprint.

 740

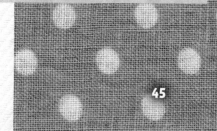

One of the most interesting but hard-to-find backprints is the "Kitchen Merry-go-Round Apron." Notice the characters: Susie Kent, Percy Kent, Baby Kent and Pussy Kent. This sack held 100 lbs. of Kasco feed.

45

Backprint Dolls

Ask a feedsack collector to name her favorite backprint and the majority of the time the answer is "Dolls!" A lovely series of dolls, known as the Sea Island Sugar Dolls, was introduced to the public during the California Pacific International Exposition held in San Diego in 1935 and 1936. This was no ordinary exhibition. From the moment of crossing the gangplank, visitors enjoyed the island experience. Months of planning created the perfect setting, complete with wharf, a thatched roof hut, tropical plants, paper mache rock formations and more. Included was a 150-seat theater with a color moving picture of sugar cane plantations in Hawaii. A favorite attraction with young ones was the puppet show telling the story of Spreckels sugar and the new Sea Island Sugar Dolls. The tired or thirsty found rest and cool drinks at the Refreshment Hut where ten cents purchased lemonade and cookies or cake. The lemonade was served unsweetened so the customer could add his own and observe how quickly Sea Island Sugar dissolved. Bags of sugar with the dolls on the back were available for purchase, as were already sewn and stuffed dolls. The exhibit was a success and drew a large percentage of the gate. It met the goal of the planners, which was to create hope in the midst of the Great Depression by sharing the latest in consumer goods.

Following are a few of the Sea Island Sugar Dolls from the J. D. and A. B. Spreckels Company, owners of Western Sugar Refinery. The dolls were released in sets such as Dolls of All Nations and the Sea Island Toys that included Little Miss Muffet, Little Red Riding Hood and others.

Dusty, The Cowboy

Chief Little Bear, The Indian

Uncle Sam

Hula, The Sea Island Dancer

47

Fifi, The French Doll

Franz, The Tyrolean Boy

Little Miss Muffet

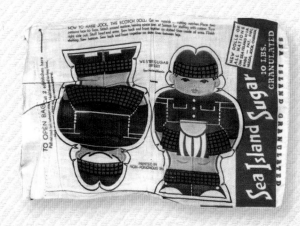

Jock, The Scotch Doll

Hulda, The Swedish Doll

Abdul, The Arabian Boy

Haru, The Japanese Girl

Tanya

48 LBS.
FLOUR

SELECTED KANSAS
HARD WHEAT

PEERLESS
HIGHEST PATENT
BLEACHED
FLOUR
.
PEERLESS FLOUR MILLS CO.
NORTON, KANSAS

48 Lbs.
Peerless Highest Patent
Bleached Flour

Bag front

A Bemis Doll

This backprint doll was made by Bemis at their Omaha facility and held 48 pounds of flour milled by the Peerless Flour Mills Co. of Norton, Kansas. It likely dates from the mid-1930s to the very early 1940s.

"Pullet Poll" Gives Edge to Truman

NOVEL PRESIDENTIAL POLL—Thomas W. Staley, general manager of the Staley Milling Co., Kansas City, is shown above with his firm's "voting sacks" of feed. Customers are expected to indicate their party preference by choosing feed sacks printed with either a donkey or an elephant on the sack band.

KANSAS CITY — First returns from the "pullet poll" being conducted among customers of the Staley Milling Co., Kansas City, show the Democrats holding a 51% to 49% lead over their Republican opponents in the affections of these poultry feed buyers in six middle and south central states.

The milling firm is packing its poultry feed in sacks with two different labels—one showing the Republican elephant and the other bearing a Democratic donkey. Dealers ask their customers which sacks they prefer and each purchase counts as a vote for the candidates of one party or the other. Dealers keep posted in their stores a day-to-day record of the local "votes" and each week the Staley company advises them of the results of the balloting

in the entire area served, comprising the states of Missouri, Kansas, Arkansas, Louisiana and parts of Nebraska and Iowa.

Local newspapers are kept informed of the trend in balloting and have given considerable publicity to the stunt.

The contest still has several weeks to run and Dewey supporters are hopeful of overtaking the lead built up in the past fortnight by the Truman backers.

RALSTON PURINA BUYS MIAMI, FLA., FEED FIRM

ST. LOUIS, MO.—The Ralston Purina Co. has acquired the feed interests and feed manufacturing facilities of the Miami (Fla.) Feed & Supply Co. in a transaction to become

― Chapter Three. ―
The 1940s: War, Peace and a Presidential Election

The 1940s opened with good news in agriculture. Farmers in Kansas were thrilled when heavy snow blanketed much of the state in January. Hopes were raised for this to mark the end of the drought. The summer months were dry in the plains, but by the end of the year, precipitation increased and continued into the next. The Dust Bowl days were finally over.

The Great Depression lingered as political tension increased in Europe. Nazi Germany invaded Poland on September 1, 1939, and nations around the globe were drawn into the conflict. World War II had begun. Germany, Italy and Japan joined forces as the Axis powers. France and Great Britain united against them. President Roosevelt chose to keep the United States out of a formal declaration of war. His programs to end the depression were showing steady progress, and war could damage his chance of winning an unprecedented third term the following year. With memories of World War 1 still fresh, American voters were firmly opposed to siding with any nation. Time was needed to increase the defense budget and win the public's approval for war. That changed on December 7, 1941, when Japan attacked Pearl Harbor. The United States declared war on Japan and sided with the

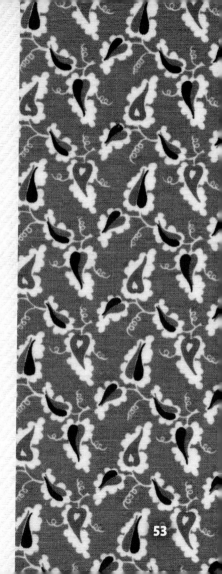

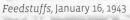

Feedstuffs, January 16, 1943

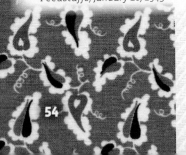

Soviet Union and Great Britain to form the Big Three among the Allied powers. A mighty nation was again at war.

Almost overnight, American industry shifted from products related to family and peace to those of war. This proved to be the jump-start the economy needed to bring an end to the Great Depression.

War Brings Fabric Restrictions

American fashion changed during World War II. Hosiery, jewelry, clothing, shoes, makeup and other items were affected. The raw material used to make artificial dyes was also needed in the manufacture of dynamite for the military. Its use in fabrics was not considered vital and women were encouraged to "make do" with undyed fabrics. Clothing styles were simplified to help in the war effort. In *No Ordinary Time*, Doris Kearns Goodwin says the army was in urgent need of the cotton and wool necessary for 165 million coats, 64 million flannel shirts and 229 million pairs of trousers. To outfit the troops, it was vital that not one yard be wasted on civilian apparel.

The War Production Board issued Order L-85 with specific instructions on garment construction. Here are a few of the restrictions faced when buying a new garment during World War II:

Women's blouses and coats were made without French cuffs, double yokes or back pleats. An attached hood or scarf was banned. A single pocket was allowed.

Fully pleated skirts were prohibited. Some variance was allowed in the sweep of the skirt, with most styles and fabrics limited to no more than seventy-two to seventy-eight inches. The maximum hem depth was two inches.

The finished length of a woman's suit jacket could not exceed twenty-five inches. It was determined this would result in an attractive silhouette with the jacket falling along the hip line for many women.

Women's pants were designed with care to help conserve precious fabric. The circumference of the hemline was restricted to a maximum of nineteen inches.

Men's double-breasted suits were banned. The single-breasted suit was required to have a narrow lapel and could not include a vest. Trousers could no longer have cuffs or pleats.

One restriction accepted with a smile had to do with bathing suits. The cloth allowed for them was reduced by ten percent. The wearing of skimpier, two piece swimwear could finally be justified as a patriotic duty.

● THEY MADE THEIR DRESSES OUT OF BAGS ●

C. L. Garrett, owner of the Farmer's Produce Co., Rogers, Ark., has been curious for some time to see just what the wives of his customers could do with some of the bags he has been obtaining from the Bemis Bros. Bag Co. in which to pack his feed. At a meeting of a club to which he and his wife belong, which includes as members a number of his customers, Mr. Garrett made arrangements to have the women wear dresses made from the bags.

The above illustration shows the results and testifies to the ingenuity of the wearers.

This photo of dresses made from Bemis feedsacks ran in a milling periodical the day before the attack on Pearl Harbor. The luxury of using this much fabric in a single dress would soon be a memory.
Feedstuffs, December 6, 1941

SEWING WITH *Cotton Bags*

(Revised edition, June 1937)

Interior of booklet:

From November 1942 to January 1943, the War Production Board issued Order M-221 that set limits on the size of feedsacks. Size referred to the poundage of the product. Before this time, sacks were available in many different sizes, such as 1, 3, 6, 9.8, 12, 24, 24.5, 48, 49, and 98 pounds. The new arrangement allowed for six sizes: 2, 5, 10, 25, 50 and 100 pounds or over. Exceptions were granted for cement, plaster, potatoes and seed. The Order stated, "The purpose of such standardization is to relieve bag manufacturers and users from the necessity of carrying an inventory of many different types and weights of paper, textiles and bags, thereby saving manpower and operating facilities." An hour saved was an hour that could be used elsewhere. It was part of the cost saving effort to help win the war.

Sewing with Cotton Bags from the Textile Bag Manufacturers Association was printed before the WPB standardized bag sizes. It states the approximate dimensions of the cloth used to hold 6, 12, 24, 49, and 98 pounds of flour. Only one entry is given for feed at 100 pounds.

The opening page of *A Bag of Tricks for Home Sewing* (on page 57) from the National Cotton Council begins with "A yard saved is a yard gained, for victory!

The war has taught us that it isn't *how much we have* that counts but *how well we use what we have.*" Demand for the booklet was

so great, plans were made to print an additional 1,000,000 copies for distribution in 1945.

First Printing, 1944

Approximate Amount of Material in Various Bags:

Flour Bags:

- 5 lb.   15" X 19"
- 10 lb.   18" X 23"
- 25 lb.   26" X 26"
- 50 lb.   30" X 34"
- 100 lb. 36" X 42"

Sugar Bags:

- 5 lb.   13" X 16"
- 10 lb.   16" X 21"
- 25 lb.   22" X 27"
- 100 lb. 36" X 40"

Salt Bags:

- 5 lb.   13" X 14"
- 10 lb.   16" X 17"
- 25 lb.   18" X 26"
- 100 lb. 30" X 36"

Meal Bags:

- 5 lb.   15" X 16"
- 10 lb.   18" X 22"
- 25 lb.   26" X 27"
- 100 lb. 36" X 44"

Feed Bags:

- 50 lb.   34" x 38.5"
- 100 lb. 39" X 46"
- 100 lb. 39" X 48"
- 100 lb. 39" X 50"
- 100 lb. 39" X 52"
- 100 lb. 39" X 54"

Fertilizer Bags:

- 100 lb. 36" X 39"
- 125 lb. 36" X 45"
- 150 lb. 39" X 44"
- 200 lb. 39" X 52"

The depression saying, "Use it up, wear it out, make it do, or do without!" took on new meaning during World War II. Instead of having little money to purchase available products, the consumer was more often in the situation of having the cash but no product

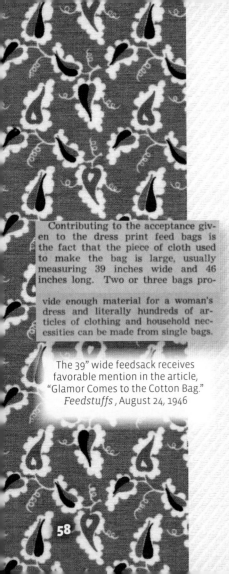

Contributing to the acceptance given to the dress print feed bags is the fact that the piece of cloth used to make the bag is large, usually measuring 39 inches wide and 46 inches long. Two or three bags provide enough material for a woman's dress and literally hundreds of articles of clothing and household necessities can be made from single bags.

The 39" wide feedsack receives favorable mention in the article, "Glamor Comes to the Cotton Bag." *Feedstuffs* , August 24, 1946

to purchase. It became a challenge to find yard goods. To help us understand what that was like, Nell Scoggins of Sequoyah County, Oklahoma, would like to share her story:

I was just a young girl when the war started and remember what we went through to buy a few yards of cotton. Before then, we could buy fabric any time but that changed and we had to wait until a shipment came in, then stand in line to buy it. We had gotten news that one of the stores would have fabric on a certain day and I knew how important it was to be there. We lived about ten miles from town and rode back and forth on the mail bus that went from Bunch to Sallisaw, so I made plans to get up early and take the bus to my aunt's house in town. When I walked to the store, the line was out the door and around the corner. I waited and waited for what must have been three hours before my turn came. We were allowed only four yards with no choice of print or color. It was take it or do without. I took it. I can't recall the design, or if it was red, blue or another color. The color didn't matter. The important thing was the cloth.

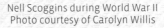

Nell Scoggins during World War II
Photo courtesy of Carolyn Willis

58

It's little wonder the dress print bags were in high demand during World War II. They satisfied an urgent need for cloth and helped brighten many a wardrobe.

We read earlier about the "bag parties" held in McCurtain County, Oklahoma, so the women could exchange sack prints. These parties were not limited to Oklahoma and by 1945, they made news in the *Kansas City Times*[3] and the milling periodical *Feedstuffs*:

"A new woman's club has popped up, the Sack and Snack Club," announces Opal H. Melton in the Cooper County Record. "It is composed of farm women who take food and feed sacks to their meetings. They put the food together for a bountiful meal, and swap the sacks until each acquires enough of one pattern to make a dress or whatever her heart desires. The print in feed sacks is beautiful and of good quality. Doggone, I sorta wish I had some chickens or something besides a husband to feed."

[3]*Kansas City Times, May 12, 1945*

This ad ran as the war raged--
Feedstuffs, September 23, 1944

THANK YOU MISTER.. FOR THE *New Dress!*

She's a sweetheart, and one of your star salesmen, too! She's all decked out in a brand new dress made from the cotton bags in which you pack your product.

Mother has learned that cotton bags can be converted into many attractive things to wear . . . that cotton bags provide a ready source of sturdy material for home sewing.

National advertising in farm publications, in domi-nant home economics magazines, in 2,800 small-town newspapers, is increasing the interest of mothers all over America in sewing with cotton bags. It is build-ing their preference for cotton-bagged products.

Tens of thousands of requests are being received for the 32-page pattern book, "Bag of Tricks for Home Sewing," which shows things to make from cotton bags. Many teachers are making the booklet a part of their classroom sewing study.

 *You can profit* . . . . .

by calling attention to this booklet in your own advertising if you are now packing your product in cotton bags. If you are not using cotton bags, talk to your bag manu-facturer immediately—ask him for a copy of the booklet, and full information on how you may tie-in with this program, or write

NATIONAL COTTON COUNCIL of AMERICA

MEMPHIS 1   P.O. Box 18   TENNESSEE

Meet the "Sack and Snack Club"
Feedstuffs, July 21, 1945

The popularity of dress print bags continued to increase with an astounding number of bags sold during the war years. The article, "Glamor Comes to the Cotton Bag," makes an interesting comparison between the total number of bags sold and the dresses that could be made from them:

Approximately 100,000,000 dress print bags were delivered by bag manufacturers last year and purchasers of commercial formula feeds and flour registered a tremendous popular approval of the merchandising technique that gives them a premium in cloth.

The demand for dress print bags was probably abnormally increased by the shortage of piece goods in dry goods stores during the past few years. At no time during the war period was the bag industry able to furnish all of the bags of this kind that were requested by the trade.

But during 1945 alone the total yardage that went into the making of flour, feed, sugar, meal and other sacks for staple products would provide approximately five dresses for every woman and girl in the United States.

When bolt goods are freely available again in the stores, some of the consumer demand for dress print bags may be dissipated. But leaders in the industry are expecting that women who have learned the economy of dresses made from dress print bags will continue to demand them. They are predicting that a major part of total production of formula feed will continue to be packed in dress print bags for many years to come.

"Cloth of the United Nations"

The Percy Kent Bag Company made an historic feedsack during this time and named it "Kent's Cloth of the United Nations." It displayed the names of early members of the United Nations and some of the events, individuals and battles significant in the history of World War II. Well before it became an official organization, representatives from twenty-six Allied nations met in Washington, D.C. to sign a "Declaration by United Nations." Twenty-five of them are named on the sack. A small number who joined later are also recorded.

A few scenes from Kent's Cloth are Guadalcanal, the Atlantic Charter, the Rock of Gibraltar, Pearl Harbor, Miracle at Dunkerque and the R.A.F. and the Battle for Britain.

THE *Designer* BEHIND THE DESIGN

There's a good reason why Ken-Print Bags are outstanding.

It's A. Charles Barton, Design Director for the Percy Kent Bag Company. From his studio in New York, Mr. Barton, one of America's foremost designers, sends out the distinctive ideas for which P/K Bags are famous.

European by birth and education, he has won wide recognition in this his adopted country, and has an international reputation as one of America's foremost fabric designers. In addition to designing the popular Ken-Print patterns, Mr.

Barton teaches fabric designing at the Moore Institute of Art, Science and Industry in Philadelphia.

Mr. Barton has just recently completed a tour of the Middle West to view first hand the many uses to which Ken-Print material is being put by the versatile homemakers of this area, and to get new ideas for future P/K patterns. Upholding the Percy Kent tradition of "always something new," he promises more of the clever, colorful designs that have made Ken-Print Bags the "glamour sacks" of America.

Always Something New

PERCY KENT BAG COMPANY, INC.

Kansas City   Buffalo   New York

Peace and Plenty

In September of 1945, World War II ended and the United States again entered a period of peace.

Innovative designs for dress print bags were not a priority during the war, but now, with the fighting over, it was full steam ahead in creating new prints in bold colors. Percy Kent Bag Company hired A. Charles Barton as their Design Director. Mr. Barton was regarded as one of America's most talented fabric designers and taught at the Moore Institute of Art, Science and Industry in Philadelphia. He agreed to design feedsack prints for Percy Kent from his studio in New York. Not to be outdone, Bemis Bag Company advertised their Bemilin dress prints were "created by New York stylists."[4] Others followed suit, and within a short period of time, thousands of new feedsack prints appeared. The customer benefited as each bag company tried to outdo the other and presented what seemed to be a never-ending variety of dress and novelty prints.

[4]*Feedstuffs, April 19, 1947, page 29*

Percy Kent Introduces A. Charles Barton
Feedstuffs, February 8, 1947

An Abundance of Prints and Advertising

"Flour bag to sun suit" with P. K.'s Ken-Print bags.
Feedstuffs, November 16, 1946

"Women go for these New York fashions."
Feedstuffs, June 21, 1947

Bemilin Prints "Do Double Work"
Feedstuffs, April 12, 1947

PATTERN POLL—The Bemis Bro.' Bag Co., St. Louis, has announced that each pattern now used for cotton dress print bags has been selected by the vote of women who use these bags for home sewing. Finding that some dress print patterns were in great demand while others were less popular, Bemis sent representatives of its market research department out to let women choose the patterns they like best from artists' sketches. In the above picture an interviewer is showing a feed store customer sample patterns. Housewives have been interviewed in several states in various parts of the country, and this territory will be extended as more surveys are made, Bemis states.

Feedstuffs
April 17, 1948

Bemis Gives Women the Vote

Bemis announced in the April 17, 1948, issue of *Feedstuffs,* "that each pattern now used for cotton dress print bags has been selected by the vote of women who use these bags for home sewing. Finding that some dress print patterns were in great demand while others were less popular, Bemis sent representatives of its market research department out to let women choose the patterns they like best from artists' sketches."

Bemis uses local farm women to pick
patterns for Bemilin Dress Print Bags
Feedstuffs, September 11, 1948

Blue Ribbon Fancy Prints by
Central Bag & Burlap Co.
Feedstuffs, November 20, 1948

"New Fulton Band-Label Bag"
Feedstuffs, November 6, 1948

THIS LITTLE BAG... WENT TO MARKET

...but it didn't stay there long, because lively colors move merchandise—and fast!!! In any product—flour, feed, salt, sugar, rice, seed—manufacturers know that the customer these days looks at the package as well as the brand. This has been proved—especially with products packed in P/K Ken-Print Bags. Your customers see the difference (even when you don't) and express their preference by spending millions of dollars annually for the brands packed in P/K Ken-Print Bags.

Pioneer in the dress print bag, Percy Kent combined color and beauty of material with a sturdiness that makes P/K Ken-Print Bags invaluable in the American home today—as the "makings" of everything from dresses to draperies. Investigate P/K Ken-Print Bags for your product.

The Percy Kent Policy of "always something new" provides a never-failing source of sales-building ideas to help you merchandise your product at a profit.

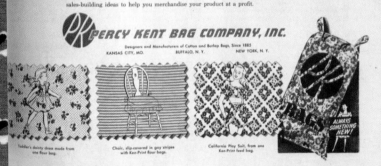

PERCY KENT BAG COMPANY, INC.

Designers and Manufacturers of Cotton and Burlap Bags, Since 1885
KANSAS CITY, MO.   BUFFALO, N. Y.   NEW YORK, N. Y.

Toddler's dainty dress made from one flour bag.

Chair, slip-covered in gay stripes with Ken-Print flour bags.

California Play Suit, from one Ken-Print feed bag.

"Always Something New"

The Percy Kent Bag Company lived up to its motto, "Always Something New," and presented beautiful new prints in the pages of milling periodicals and magazines. Here are a few from the second half of the 1940s. You may recognize prints from your own collection.

Photos courtesy of Roger D. Miller and Gateway Packaging Co., Inc.

"This Little Bag Went to Market"
Fortune, September 1946

"Containers Designed to Promote Sales"
Fortune, January 1947

"It's the container designed for re-use"
Fortune, April 1947

"Container and Premium All-in-One"
Fortune, September 1947

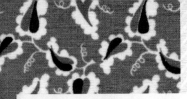

"You have to pay for a container...Why not one that smart housewives can re-use?"
Fortune, January 1948

"Two-Way Bargain in Packaging"
Fortune, March 1948

"Calico Bags and PK Has 'em!"
Fortune, November 1948

Feedsacks and the Presidential Election of 1948

Staley Milling Company of Kansas City came up with a novel idea for the 1948 presidential election. They requested the Percy Kent Bag Company make a variety of feedsack prints with either a Democratic donkey or a Republican elephant on the band label. Customers could cast a "vote" for president by choosing a sack from the desired party. Each purchase counted as one vote. Early results from the "pullet poll" were announced in the milling periodical *Feedstuffs*:

"Pullet Poll" Gives Edge to Truman

First returns from the "pullet poll" being conducted among customers of the Staley Milling Co., Kansas City, show the Democrats holding a 51% to 49% lead over their Republican opponents in the affections of these poultry feed buyers in six middle and south central states.

The milling firm is packing its poultry feed in sacks with two different labels--one showing the Republican elephant and the other bearing a Democratic donkey. Dealers ask their customers which sacks they prefer and each purchase counts as a vote for the candidates of one party or the other. Dealers keep posted in their stores a day-to-day record of the local "votes" and each week the

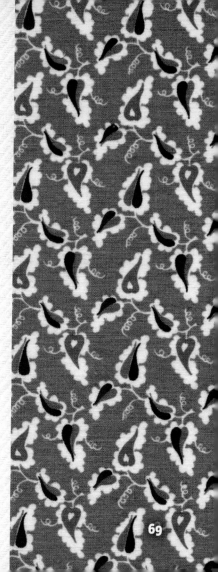

"Pullet Poll" Gives Edge to Truman

NOVEL PRESIDENTIAL POLL—Thomas W. Staley, general manager of the Staley Milling Co., Kansas City, is shown above with his firm's "voting sacks" of feed. Customers are expected to indicate their party preference by choosing feed sacks printed with either a donkey or an elephant on the sack band.

KANSAS CITY — First returns from the "pullet poll" being conducted among customers of the Staley Milling Co., Kansas City, show the Democrats holding a 51% to 49% lead over their Republican opponents in the affections of these poultry feed buyers in six middle and south central states.

The milling firm is packing its poultry feed in sacks with two different labels—one showing the Republican elephant and the other bearing a Democratic donkey. Dealers ask their customers which sacks they prefer and each purchase counts as a vote for the candidates of one party or the other. Dealers keep posted in their stores a day-to-day record of the local "votes" and each week the Staley company advises them of the results of the balloting

in the entire area served, comprising the states of Missouri, Kansas, Arkansas, Louisiana and parts of Nebraska and Iowa.

Local newspapers are kept informed of the trend in balloting and have given considerable publicity to the stunt.

The contest still has several weeks to run and Dewey supporters are hopeful of overtaking the lead built up in the past fortnight by the Truman backers.

RALSTON PURINA BUYS MIAMI, FLA., FEED FIRM

ST. LOUIS, MO.—The Ralston Purina Co. has acquired the feed interests and feed manufacturing facilities of the Miami (Fla.) Feed & Supply Co. in a transaction to become

A variety of sack prints were used in the Staley Poll.
Feedstuffs, September 4, 1948

Staley company advises them of the results of the balloting in the entire area served, comprising the states of Missouri, Kansas, Arkansas, Louisiana and parts of Nebraska and Iowa.

Local newspapers are kept informed of the trend in balloting and have given considerable publicity to the stunt.

The contest still has several weeks to run and Dewey supporters are hopeful of overtaking the lead built up in the past fortnight by the Truman backers.

Thomas W. Staley, general manager of the Staley Milling Co., Kansas City, is shown with his firm's 'voting sacks' of feed. Customers are expected to indicate their party preference by choosing feed sacks printed with either a donkey or an elephant on the sack band.

To the surprise of many, votes for the Democrats climbed even higher in the "pullet poll" with a 54% to 46% preference for Harry S. Truman. At this point, the poll was discontinued as too unlikely. The Republican candidate, Thomas E. Dewey had strong backing from the unionized east, and it was widely believed this guaranteed his win. Democrats suddenly courted farmers and ranchers, who received little consideration from the Republicans. Truman began a 30,000-mile whistlestop tour with the goal of reaching everyday families from the farm belt to cattle country. He spoke to the crowds as a trusted friend and gave them hope for higher farm prices and wages. Women were reminded they held power in the election and should vote with the education of their children in mind. When the election results came in, Truman received 49.6% of the popular vote to Dewey's 45.1% and won the electoral vote by a landslide of 303 to 189. It has been called "the greatest upset in the history of American politics."[5]

[5] "Presidential Politics," American Experience, http://www.pbs.org/wgbh/amex/truman/sfeature/sf_ppolitics.html

Staley Poll Picks the Winner
★ ★ ★   ★ ★ ★
Forecast Gave Truman 8% Vote Margin

KANSAS CITY—One of the very few polls to correctly catch the trend in the farm vote, which won the presidential election for the Democrats, was the Staley Milling Co.'s customers' poll on its poultry feed sales.

With special labels depicting the Democratic donkey and Republican elephant on poultry feed sacks, the Staley firm invited customers to choose the sack with the label of their political preference. Tabulation of votes thus expressed was kept on display in the dealer's store, the changes being made each week.

President Truman jumped into a modest lead at the start of the poll and maintained his advantage throughout. The final vote percentages, 54% for Truman and 46% for Dewey were pretty close to the actual results of the election.

Thomas W. Staley, general manager of the company, said there is no truth to the rumor that Elmo Roper and George Gallup, professional pollsters, and various and sundry politicians of both parties, were offering high prices for an explanation of the Staley Poll technique.

Feedstuffs, November 6, 1948

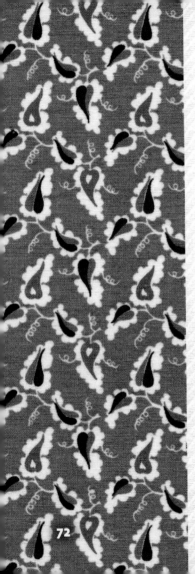

The purchase of this "gardening man" feedsack in bright Crayola colors was a vote for the Democrats and Truman.

Inauguration Button for
Harry S. Truman
January 20, 1949

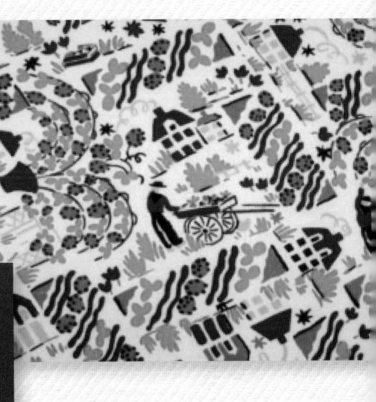

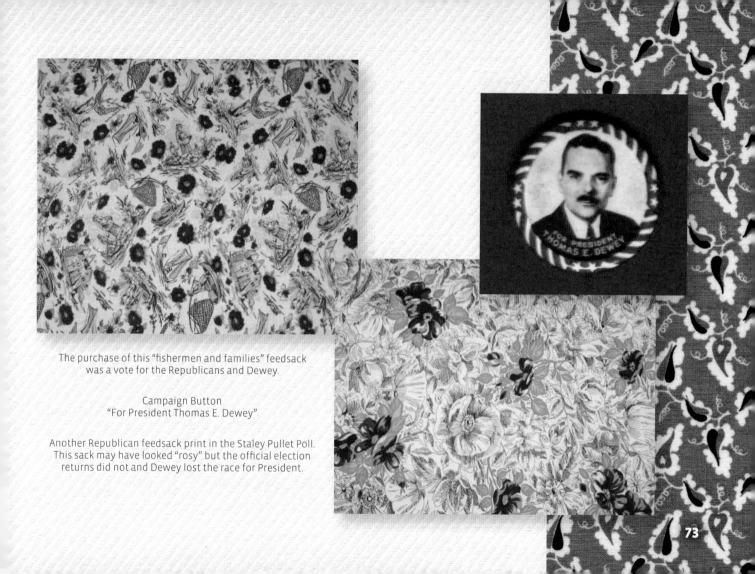

The purchase of this "fishermen and families" feedsack was a vote for the Republicans and Dewey.

Campaign Button
"For President Thomas E. Dewey"

Another Republican feedsack print in the Staley Pullet Poll. This sack may have looked "rosy" but the official election returns did not and Dewey lost the race for President.

The Zipper Feedbag

In May 1949, a new feature in dress print bags was introduced by Pay Way Feeds of Kansas City. Their bags of Extra Rich Growing Granules would now include a 9" Talon zipper, valued at 30 cents. "Just think of all the things you can make using beautiful Pay Way prints and Talon zippers…"

Feedstuffs
May 21, 1949

INTRODUCE NEW BAG—Launching a campaign to market Pay Way feeds in zipper bags was the above group which met at the Hotel Continental in Kansas City May 7. The zipper now is included with the dress print packaging of feeds produced by the Pay Way Feed Mills, Inc., Kansas City. Left to right around the table are Edward Segrist, account executive for Potts, Calkins & Holden Advertising Co.; Larry Alley, traffic manager, Pay Way Feed Mills, Inc.; C. H. Buckey, Missouri sales-man; W. Q. Johnson, Minnesota salesman; Oscar M. Straube, president of the company; J. L. Barrick, advertising manager of the Weekly Kansas City Star; Fred Newman, Missouri salesman; J. W. Banister, advertising manager; John J. Clay, sales supervisor; L. S. Darland, Kansas salesman; B. B. Hoffine, credit manager; D. E. Moore, nutritionist; C. L. Browne, Missouri salesman; Loren G. Land, Missouri salesman; John Gross, Missouri salesman, and Wilbur A. Burke, Kansas salesman.

Businessmen meet at the Hotel Continental in Kansas City on May 7, 1949, to discuss the campaign to market Pay Way feeds in zipper bags. Present at the meeting was J. L. Barrick, advertising manager for the *Weekly Kansas City Star*.
Feedstuffs, May 21, 1949

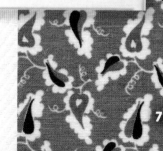

Betty Bemis, Phil Fawn and Teddy Bear
The Feed Bag, November 1949
Photo courtesy Bemis Company, Inc.

Doll and Toy Feedsacks from the Late 1940s

The Bemis Bag Company introduced "cut-outs" in the late 1940s. Meet Betty Bemis, Phil Fawn, and Teddy Bear designed by New York artists. Cutting lines and easy-to-follow instructions printed right on the bag meant a new toy for baby in a matter of minutes.

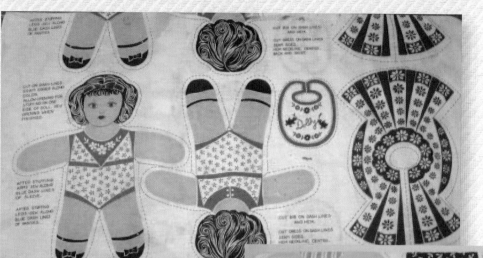

Betty Bemis Sack

Teddy Bear Sack

Chapter Four.
Feedsack Cartoons

Feedsack cartoons were an occasional feature in milling periodicals. More than half a century has passed since they appeared, and they still bring a chuckle to feedsack lovers everywhere.

"There's the most eligible bachelor in this county. He has over two hundred empty ERWIN prints!"

Feedstuffs,
June 5, 1948

(left) Cartoons from *Feedstuffs.* Clockwise from upper left, the issues are: February 2, 1952; November 10, 1951; December 31, 1949; December 20, 1947, January 3, 1948.

"It looks like fine feed, but our flock is used to feed in dress-print bags."

SUPER CHICKEN FEED

POWER FULL CHICKY FOOD

Feed Illustrated,
March, 1952
Photo courtesy The National Provisioner.

Feeds Illustrated, February 1953
Photo courtesy The
National Provisioner

Feeds Illustrated, August 1954
Photo courtesy The National Provisioner

"Does this pattern do anything for me?"

Feeds Illustrated
February 1955
Photo courtesy The
National Provisioner

"Copy Cat!"

Feeds Illustrated
December 1957
Photo courtesy The
National Provisioner

"Junior! You be careful with that ERWIN print bag!"

Feedstuffs, July 17, 1948

"We're getting ten times as much to eat since his wife saw those ERWIN print feed bags."

Feedstuffs, January 30, 1948

"Don't think you're going to fill up this trunk with your old stocks and bonds!"

Feedstuffs, January 15, 1949

"Are you sure you're not just temporarily dazzled by my **ERWIN** print dress?"

Feedstuffs, July 31, 1948

"Fowl Fashion Show" Planned

PENB Promotion Features Feed Bags

CHICAGO—A "Fowl Fashion Show," a search for a new kind of "look" designed to put fashions "in the bag"—poultry feed bags, that is —and concentrate nation-wide attention on poultry products, is the latest promotion of the Poultry & Egg National Board.

The new campaign to publicize poultry—in one of the biggest production seasons on record — calls for a contest to find the 10 "best-dressed" fowl in the nation. The fowl will be "dressed" in costumes designed and made from poultry feed-bag material and exhibited — in typical fashion-parade style—on live chickens, ducks or turkeys.

Costumes will be judged on originality of design, fit and workman-ship. Grand prize is a Kaiser "Traveler" automobile.

Open to the general public, the contest starts this month and terminates with a grand finale at the fact-finding conference of the Institute of American Poultry Industries in Kansas City in February.

The national winner will be selected through a process of state and regional eliminations. State contest winners will compete in regional elimination contests. Two winners will be selected from each of five regions. The regions are: northeastern, north central, south central and western.

The regional winners—the "10 best-dressed fowl in the nation"—will compete at Kansas City for the national

title: "the best-dressed fowl ... Creator of the winning costume ... be awarded the Kaiser automo...

"The fowl fashion promotion ... a very effective peg on which ... nationwide publicity for our ... and its products," said the co-sa... Berger, pres..., American F... Manufacture... Assn., and Ho... Huntingto... PENB gener... manager.

In commenting further on the promotion, Mr. Berger said:

"The contest of...fers promotions ... all segments of our industry. Every...body can get in on this 'act' and the publicity potentials are terrific.

"Serving on the national committee, in addition to Mr. Berger and Mr. Huntington, are: Dr. Cliff Carpenter, president, Institute of American Poultry Industries; Don Turnbull, executive secretary; International Baby Chick Assn., and Ray Bowden, executive vice president, Grain & Feed Dealers National Assn.

"Promotion tie-in plans and suggestions have been released to all members of the feed manufacturers' and dealers' associations, International Baby Chick Assn., the institute, other organization members of PENB and 4,600 Kaiser-Frazer dealer agencies. Many of these organizations and their members already have indicated their will cooperate in the campaign and have set promotion wheels in motion, the board points out.

"Five- or six-man committees have been appointed in each state. State committees will be charged with the responsibility of localizing the Fowl Fashion Show and conducting the state elimination judging contests.

"In the Fowl Fashion Show we have a contest that should arouse the interest of every news and photo editor in the country," Mr. Huntington observed.

"An extensive exploitation job on this contest on the part of everyone connected with the poultry industry," he added, "is bound to result in tremendous publicity impact for our industry's products—and that impact will come during one of the biggest poultry crops in history."

Further information on the promotion may be obtained from the Poultry & Egg National Board, 306 W. Washington St., Chicago 6, Ill.

Charles Darwin found in his experiments with earthworms that ... fertile the soil they ...

Ducy Duck

Tula Turkey

Rudy Rooster

Busy-Body Biddy

Chapter Five.
The 1950s: Susie-Q and a Decade of Contests

Farm wives were excited about an announcement in the September 3, 1949, issue of *Feedstuffs*. The Poultry and Egg National Board was sponsoring a contest to find the best-dressed fowl in the nation, and the designer of the winning costume would be handed the keys to a brand new Kaiser Traveler. Valued at more than $2000, this was no ordinary vehicle. The Traveler boasted an innovative hatchback, comfortable seats, a quiet ride and a spacious cargo area. With the look of a sedan and the carrying capacity of a utility vehicle, the Kaiser Traveler lived up to its name, "the world's most useful car," and women everywhere hoped to win it.[6]

One of the rules of the contest stated all garments must be "designed and made from poultry feed-bag material and exhibited -- in typical fashion-parade style -- on live chickens, ducks or turkeys." The goal was to create nationwide interest in the poultry industry and its products during "one of the biggest poultry crops in history."

[6]*"America on the Move,"* National Museum of American History, http://americanhistory.si.edu/onthemove/collection/object_613.html

Fulprint Bags Designed for Your Customer's Re-Use
Fulton Fulprint
Feed Age, June 1952
Photo courtesy of Fulton Denver Company

"Fowl Fashion Show" Planned
Feedstuffs, September 3, 1949

Rudy Rooster

Busy-Body Biddy

Ducy Duck

Tula Turkey

The announcement "Fowl Fashion Show Planned," explained how the winner would be chosen:

> Costumes will be judged on originality of design, fit and workmanship. Grand prize is a Kaiser "Traveler" automobile.
>
> Open to the general public, the contest starts this month and terminates with a grand finale at the fact-finding conference of the Institute of American Poultry Industries in Kansas City in February.
>
> The national winner will be selected through a process of state and regional elimination judging contests. State contest winners will compete in regional elimination contests. Two winners will be selected from each of five regions. The regions are: northeastern, southeastern, north central, south central and western.
>
> The regional winners -- the "10 best-dressed fowl in the nation" -- will compete at Kansas City for the national title: "the best-dressed fowl of 1950." Creator of the winning costume will be awarded the Kaiser automobile.

Costumes were imaginative and well made. At the state competition, the

JUST DUCKY—All decked out in its poultry feed bag costume, this duck has its bonnet adjusted by Mary Lou Prentice, pretty model, at the Preview Fowl Fashion Show staged recently by the Poultry & Egg National Board at the Quaker Oats Co. farm, Libertyville, Ill. For the benefit of newsmen and major photo syndicates, both human and barnyard models displayed the costumes made from feed bags.

Just Ducky
Preview Fowl Fashion Show
Feedstuffs, October 8, 1949

Kentucky winner wore "a flowered print dress with matching bonnet and parasol." She had nothing on Tom Turkey from Minnesota. He sported "green trousers, white shirt, high wing collar with a flowered bow tie and high hat." Frills and finery were seen in the "elaborate Victorian ensemble" modeled by the Illinois entry. The two winners from the southeastern region wore south-of-the-border, rhumba costumes. One of the winners of the western region was Oscar the rooster who dressed in bright colored trousers with matching suspenders, a light colored shirt and a big bow tie. Oscar was interviewed in Salt Lake City just prior to leaving for the national competition and declared to be a "dapper little bird" who "struts cockily."

PENB FOWL FASHION SHOW—Winners from four states in the "fowl fashion show" being sponsored by the Poultry & Egg National Board are shown in the illustration above. At the left is the Minnesota winner, entered by Mrs. Ben Terhard, Rushmore; an outfit for "Tom" complete with green trousers, white shirt, high wing collar with a flowered bow tie and high hat. Left center, the Illinois entry, with an elaborate Victorian ensemble, entered by Mrs. Roy L. Davis, Elwood. Right center, the Kentucky winner, wearing a flowered print dress with matching bonnet and parasol. The costume was designed by Mrs. C. H. Ray, Elizabethtown, and the bird is held by Patricia Stevens, head of the modeling agency bearing her name and a contest judge. In the illustration at the right is the Indiana winner entered by Mrs. C. L. A. Miller, Mishawaka, held by Grace Miller, Christian Science Monitor, one of the judges.

Groomed from beak to tail feathers and modeling the finest in feedsack wear, the ten regional winners gathered in Kansas City, Missouri, in February of 1950 for the grand finale. The title of "Best Dressed Fowl of 1950" went to Susie-Q, who impressed the judges in a lovely "French ensemble of the 1830 era" sewn from a Bemilin bag. Her owners, Mr. and Mrs. John Riffle of Shenandoah, Iowa, posed for photographs with Susie-Q as they accepted their new Kaiser Traveler.

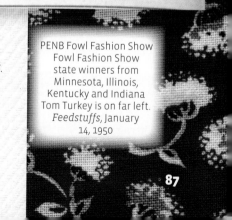

PENB Fowl Fashion Show Fowl Fashion Show state winners from Minnesota, Illinois, Kentucky and Indiana Tom Turkey is on far left. *Feedstuffs*, January 14, 1950

FOWL FASHIONS—Several feed men who attended the recent Indiana Grain & Feed Dealers Assn. convention were pressed into service as attendants for the birds entered in the Fowl Fashion Show put on by the Poultry & Egg National Board. Pictured, left to right, are: Jo Watson, PENB publicity director, who emceed the show; Dorwin Franks, Rudy Klausmeire, Ezra Stoler, Tom Bash, Art Goeglenn (almost hidden), Walter Creek, Kaywood VanNote, Paul Whitacre, Denver Wilson and Vern Steckley.

Fowl Fashions
Feed men attending the convention of the Indiana Grain & Feed Dealers Association attend to birds entered in the Fowl Fashion Show.
Feedstuffs, February 18, 1950

BEST DRESSED FOWL—The "best dressed fowl of 1950," Susie Q. Riffle, is held by the owner and costume designer, Mrs. John Riffle of the John Riffle Hatchery, Shenandoah, Iowa. Mrs. Riffle is seated on the Kaiser Traveler automobile which she won as the grand prize in the Fowl Fashion Show sponsored by the Poultry & Egg National Board at the recent Mid-Century Fact Finding Conference of the Institute of American Poultry Industries at Kansas City. Walter C. Berger (right), president of the American Feed Manufacturers Assn. and chairman of the Fowl Fashion Show National Committee, and Jo Watson (left of Mrs. Riffle), PENB publicity director and emcee of the contest finals, examine the winning costume, a French ensemble of the 1830 era. Homer Huntington, PENB general manager, looks on. Susie Q.'s costume won over nine other regional winners.

Susie Q, "Best Dressed Fowl of 1950"
Feedstuffs, March 4, 1950

Susie-Q, "The Pride of John Riffle Hatchery"
Feeds Illustrated, May 1951
Photo courtesy of The National Provisioner

Percy Kent Introduces Walt Disney Prints

1950 was a great year for feedsack prints. Walt Disney Productions granted the Percy Kent Bag Company of Kansas City the exclusive right to print Walt Disney characters "on quality cotton materials" in designs specifically created for them by the Walt Disney Studios. By July of 1950, Mickey Mouse, Donald Duck, Pluto and other Disney characters were added to the Ken-Prints line "in a variety of designs and colors." The prints were also featured in "ready-to-use apron bags -- complete with drawstring and attractive ruffled top."

Quality percales were used for the Walt Disney prints. Doughboy Industries, Inc. of New Richmond, Wisconsin, advertised their Premium Poultry Feeds were *"sacked in 80-square percales starring favorite Walt Disney characters: Mickey Mouse, Donald Duck and Pluto. Remember... in the entire Upper Midwest only Doughboy sacks its Poultry Feeds in strong, smooth, 80-square percales!"*

"Disney Figures Romp on Cotton Bags"
Feedstuffs, July 1, 1950

Disney Figures Romp on Cotton Bags

KANSAS CITY—Famous Walt Disney characters are now appearing on "Ken-Print" cotton bags for flour produced by the Percy Kent Bag Co. Richard K. Peek, president of the bag manufacturing company, said that special arrangements had been concluded with Walt Disney Produc-

tions for the exclusive right to print on quality cotton materials copyrighted Walt Disney characters in designs created for the bag company by the Walt Disney studios.

Mickey Mouse, Donald Duck, Pluto and other members of Walt Disney's rollicking crew are available in a variety of designs and colors. Walt Disney Ken-Prints also will be available in all standard bag sizes that bring cotton material ready to cut into sun-suits and rompers for youngsters or dress-ups for the home.

Percy-Kent is also featuring Walt Disney Ken-Prints in its ready-to-use apron bags—complete with drawstring and attractive ruffled top.

The merchandising appeal of the Walt Disney characters is the newest addition to the extensive line developed by the Percy Kent Bag Co. in the design and manufacture of print cotton bags of the container and premium combination type for a wide variety of products. It is estimated that a majority of the prize-winning garments shown at county fairs are now made of print materials from flour and feed bags.

MERGER ANNOUNCED

SAGINAW, MICH.—The merger of Charles Wolohan, Inc., operator of seven grain elevators in the Saginaw area, and the Wickes Corp. of Saginaw, owner of three other industrial plants, was announced June 9. The Wolohan firm has a capacity of 365,000 bu. Stockholders of both firms approved the merger. The merger gives Wickes 50% ownership of Saginaw Grain Co., recently organized to finance construction of a 1-million bushel elevator. Robert E. Wolohan, vice president and general manager of the Wolohan firm, becomes a vice president of Wickes and general manager of its Wolohan division.

PurAsnow Flour was also packaged in fine quality, 80-square percale prints. The Percy Kent Bag Company made the sacks.

"Southern Mansions" on a snow white background

"Spirit of 1776" with an antique ivory background

THIS IS Fine Quality 80·80 Percale
WASH FAST COLORS
Wonderful for Home Sewing
FULL SQUARE YARD

PurAsnow
PurAsnow 25 LB. NET
ENRICHED SELF-RISING FLOUR
PurAsnow
15¢ OFF

The Percy Kent Bag Company advertised another new feedsack style in August of 1950. It was the hemmed and ready to use luncheon cloth. Notice the 59-cent retail value printed on the label.

Pretty Prints and Fulprints in the 1950s

Chase Bag Company named their designs Chase Pretty Prints. Their advertisements appeared in a number of milling periodicals in the early 1950s:

There's A Rainbow 'Round My Shoulders! Chase Pretty Prints *Feedstuffs* January 28, 1950

How to Make Your Flour Bloom Chase Pretty Prints *Feeds Illustrated* April 1952 Photo courtesy of The National Provisioner

Patterns Like These Are Sure To Please
Chase Pretty Prints
Feedstuffs, May 27, 1950

More and More the Perfect Score
Chase Pretty Prints
The Feed Bag, October 1952
Photo Courtesy of International Paper

Fulton Bag Company prints were called Fulton Fulprints. Here are a few of their advertisements from the early 1950s:

It's "Sew Easy" with Fulton Fulprint Cotton Bags
Fulton Fulprint Cotton Bags
Feedstuffs
January 6, 1951

It's Sew Easy with Fulton Fulprint Bags
Fulton Fulprint Cotton Bags
Feedstuffs
December 2, 1950

FULPRINT BAGS

designed

for your

customer's

RE-USE

The bright, sprightly new patterns and colors of *Fulprint* Bags are an exciting invitation for customer re-use. Easy and simple to prepare for sewing. *Fulprint* Bags offer your customers colorfast, quality cotton cloth for hundreds of home sewing uses. *Fulprint* Bags give you a sturdier, handsomer, more dependable container for your product. With production controlled from raw cotton to finished bag, you're assured of uniform quality — fashion keyed for customer appeal! Learn the entire *Fulprint* story from our nearest branch.

4 100 lb. | *Fulprint* **BAGS** | **WILL MAKE** | **THIS DRESS**

Atlanta • St. Louis • Dallas • Denver
Kansas City, Kans. • Minneapolis
New Orleans • Los Angeles
New York City, 347 Madison Ave.

Fulprint Bags Designed for Your Customer's Re-Use
Fulton Fulprint Bags
Feed Age, August 1952
Photo courtesy of Fulton Denver Company

This logo has long baffled feedsack collectors. Perhaps it stands for Fulton Fulprint.

Move Over, Rainbow
Bemis Dress Print Bags
Feedstuffs
September 27, 1952

The Bemis Company manufactured dress print bags throughout the 1950s.

You may wonder about the cat on the Bemis label. According to the company website, the original Bemis cat was named Biddy and held the position of "champion mouser" at their factory in St. Louis. She appeared on the company trademark in 1881 as a symbol that Bemis Bro. & Company had nothing to hide and dealt in an honest and fair way with all customers.

Multiwall Paper Bags

The 1950s brought change to the bag industry. Multiwall paper bags increased in popularity and began to replace dress print ones. Cost was a major factor in the switch to paper as was customer demand for smaller bags. Technological advances in the production of paper led to the opening of new, multiwall bag facilities for Werthan, Bemis, Fulton and others.

Construction of Percy Kent's new multiwall paper facility in Kansas City, Missouri, was completed by mid-1954. Although both paper and textile bags were manufactured at the plant, sales of textile bags continued to decline. In the words of the company, "A new era had begun."[7]

[7]Percy Kent Bag Company, Inc., *PK: Our First Hundred Years*, undated booklet, page 9

"The call for multiwall is the call for Fulton."
Feedstuffs, April 1, 1950

None Better
for Storing and Shipping Feeds!

QUALITY
that Costs No More
EVERY FEATURE
for Outstanding
Performance

M/W MULTIWALL PAPER BAGS

by

**CHASE
BAG**

And look to Chase, too, for burlap bags, cotton bags, smart pretty-prints. Make Chase your bag-packaging headquarters.

Multiwall Bags, like everything else, should be *right* for the job—right for *you*. Anything less wastes your time and dollars, means loss and inconvenience to customers.

That's why Chase supplies Multiwalls in such wide variety, in so many types and constructions . . . why the many Chase options—in papers, tapes, sewing—permit precise, money-saving selection.

Chase recommendations are backed by 110 years of bag-making progress . . . of service and satisfaction. It's wise to specify "Chase" for *dependable* Multiwalls—for uniformity, durability, attractive bag printing . . . reliable shipment.

CHASE BAG COMPANY

Most bag companies used paper by the time this 1958 Chase Bag ad appeared. Once the darling of the bag industry, "smart pretty prints" are mentioned in tiny lettering on the lower left.

The Feed Bag, January 1958
Photo Courtesy of International Paper

A Change in Bags and in the White House

The Staley Pullet Poll of 1952 predicted Eisenhower and the Republican Party would regain control of the White House with the "farm vote in the middle west" being a vital factor. Once again, it proved to be true. Another change is in the bag itself. Look closely and you will see these are *paper* voting bags.

Election Year Bags
Staley Pullet Poll Favors
Eisenhower
Feedstuffs, September 27, 1952

VOTERS TAKE THEIR CHOICE— Feed buyers can cast a straw vote for their presidential favorite by asking for their poultry feed with the donkey or elephant label this fall in Staley feed stores. Betty Benton of the Staley Milling Co. staff in Kansas City, holds samples of the voting bags in the picture above. Early returns from this Staley Pullet Poll reveal Gen. Eisenhower running slightly ahead of Gov. Adlai Stevenson. The general has 50.5% of the total vote so far, compared with 49.5% for the Democratic standard bearer. In the past several weeks, however, the trend has veered a bit more to the Illinois governor. In 1948, the Staley Pullet Poll proved to be one of the very few accurate straw votes. It forecast the reelection of President Truman when the scientific, high-powered pollsters were all predicting his defeat. This election-year again the farm vote in the middle west is expected to be a vital factor.

Contests in the 1950's

The 1950s was the decade of contests for the dress print bag. As paper containers gained acceptance, the National Cotton Council took action to protect its interests in cotton and keep the product in high demand with the housewife. The solution, at least for a short while, was in contests. Following are a few of the many that helped prolong the time of the patterned feedsack.

In 1953, the National Cotton Council announced a "National Cotton Bag Sewing Contest." Mrs. Esther McGugin won the title of "International Cotton Bag Sewing Queen" along with a new Pfaff sewing machine. This 1954 *Idea Book for Sewing with Cotton Bags* stated the rules for the next contest in the series, the "Save with Cotton Bags" Sewing Contest.

Three of the contests sponsored by the National Cotton Council and Textile Bag Manufacturers Association:

STYLE SHOW CRITICS—Representatives of textile bag manufacturers were interested spectators and critics at a style show staged in Minneapolis March 4 by the Textile Bag Mfrs. Assn. in connection with the annual convention of the Farmers Elevator Assn. of Minnesota. The young ladies in the picture were two of the several models who displayed the latest styles in evening dresses, fashioned from dress prints. The men in the picture, from left to right, are Oliver M. Smith, Bemis Bro. Bag Co., Minneapolis; James F. Pouchot, TBMA representative, Evanston, Ill., and George H. Christian, sales manager for the Minneapolis plant of the Chase Bag Co.

Feedstuffs
March 8, 1952

STYLE SHOW—These five models displayed attractive garments made from cotton feed bags for the wives of feed men attending the recent Indiana Grain & Feed Dealers Assn. golden anniversary convention in Indianapolis. The show arranged by the Textile Bag Manufacturers Assn., attracted considerable attention in Indianapolis newspapers. The models were loaned by a local department store. (A story about the convention appeared in the Jan. 26, 1952, issue of Feedstuffs, page 10.)

Feedstuffs
February 23, 1952

Feedstuffs
July 7, 1951

Pattern Service

FOR HER...

Sales Service

FOR YOU!

Pattern Service for Sewing with Cotton Bags is already hard at work building sales for your cotton bagged products! Advertising in leading national and regional farm publications offers this valuable booklet as a **FREE GIFT** from the manufacturer who packs in cotton bags. Heavy response indicates that more than 1,500,000 copies will be requested this year. The booklet shows farm women how to save container costs by using the cloth in cotton bags to make smart fashions and useful household items. **Pattern Service** is available in quantity on a cost-of-printing basis for direct distribution to your customers. Write today for a supply of **1952 Pattern Service for Sewing with Cotton Bags.**

Advertisement for the booklet *1952 Pattern Service for Sewing with Cotton Bags* by the National Cotton Council *Feedstuffs*, April 26, 1952

A Time for New Things

We've followed the progression of the dress print bag from its patent in 1924 through thirty years of change in color, style and pattern. By the late 1950s and early 1960s, most bag companies had completed the transition to paper for their grain products. Bemis was an exception and marketed colorful feedsacks through the 1960s.

Interest in feedsack cloth for clothing and quilting declined rapidly as the 1950s drew to a close and a new decade began. Millions of women entered the workplace and no longer had time for sewing. Those who did could find a wide range of fabrics, including new synthetics, in the local department store or through mail order catalogs. For many, it was no longer necessary to make do or do without.

A robust economy also contributed to the decline of the dress print bag. Those were the decades of family television (remember *Father Knows Best, Lassie, the Lone Ranger* and the *Dick Van Dyke Show*), big houses, bridge clubs and neighborhood parties, trips to Disneyland, and a hobby for every member of the family. New and exciting times had arrived with hope of even better days ahead. It was not with sadness the dress print bag quietly disappeared. It was simply a time for other things.

My Favorite Feedsacks

Thousands of feedsack prints were issued with flowers, ribbons, bows, cowboy scenes, plaids, stripes, polka dots, landscapes, birds, fruit, curtain prints, farm animals, children, nursery prints and more. From pastels and sherbets to bold, rich colors, feedsacks were available in a color and pattern to suit every taste. Here are a few of my favorites:

The Dodge City style print. See the women waving from the saloon balcony.

Two additional colorways of Dodge City

This Cowboy sack held twenty-five pounds of flour.

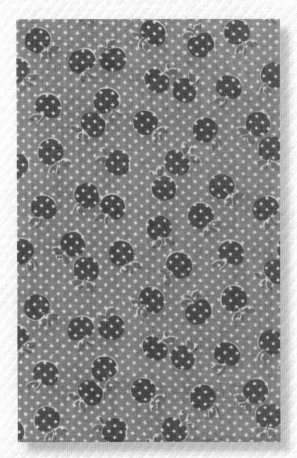

Apples

Children at Play

Shades of blue, yellow and red were popular combinations.

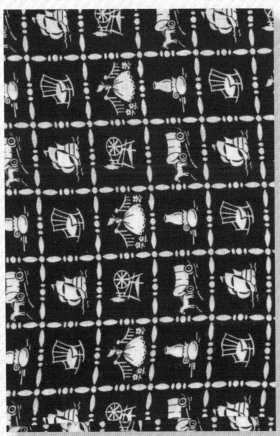

Spinning Wheel

Sailboats and Lighthouses

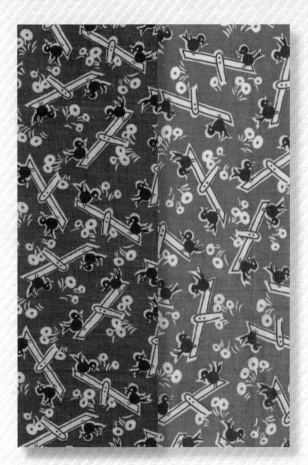

Hard-to-find Birds on a Teeter Totter in two colorways

Davy Crockett in two colorways

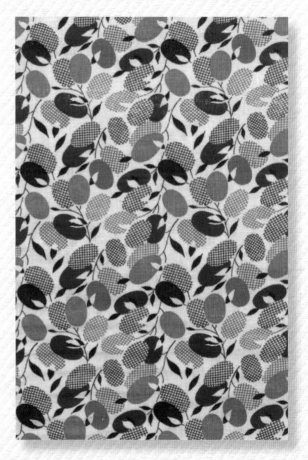

Art Deco Style

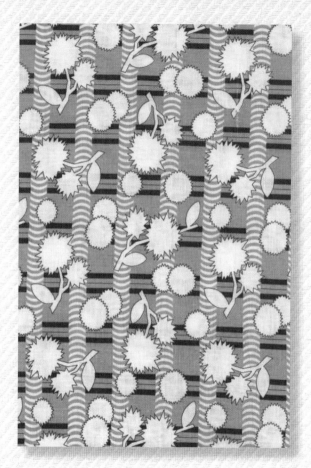

Art Deco Style

Ice Cream Soda Fountain Scene

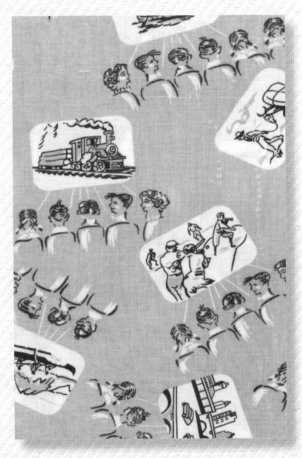

Rare feedsack print of Kids at the Movies

Cats and Dogs

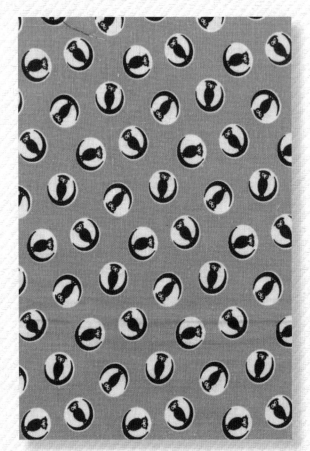

Pigs at Trough and Owl on the Crescent Moon

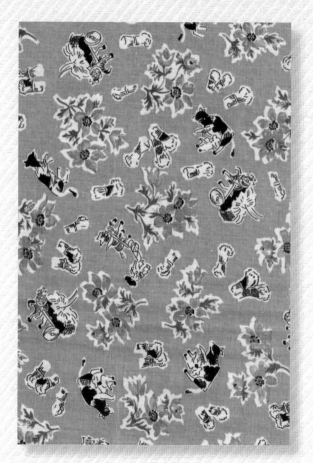

Farm Scenes and Animals

Clowns on Bright Yellow

Umbrellas

Musical Bears

Ring-Around-the-Rosy

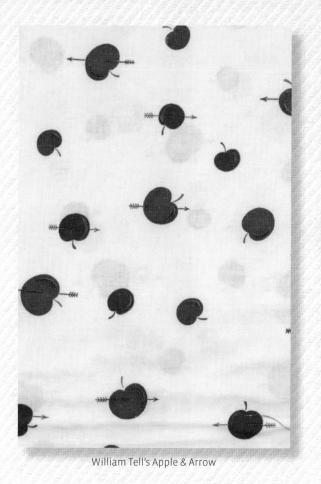

William Tell's Apple & Arrow

Ballerinas

Typical Flower and Leaf Prints

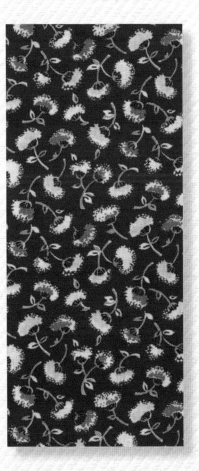

More Flower Prints

Magic Carpet

Sewing Girl

Candles and Holders

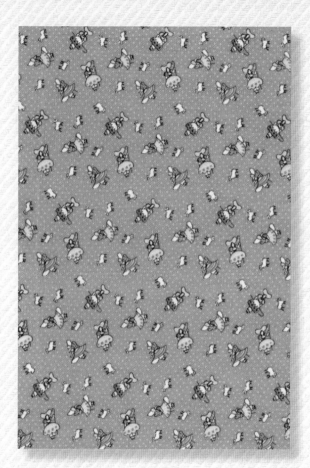

Little Bo Peep and Jack and Jill

Bright Nursery Prints

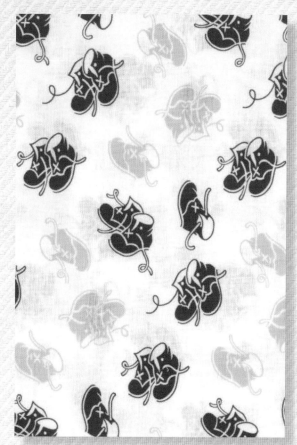

Bright Nursery Prints

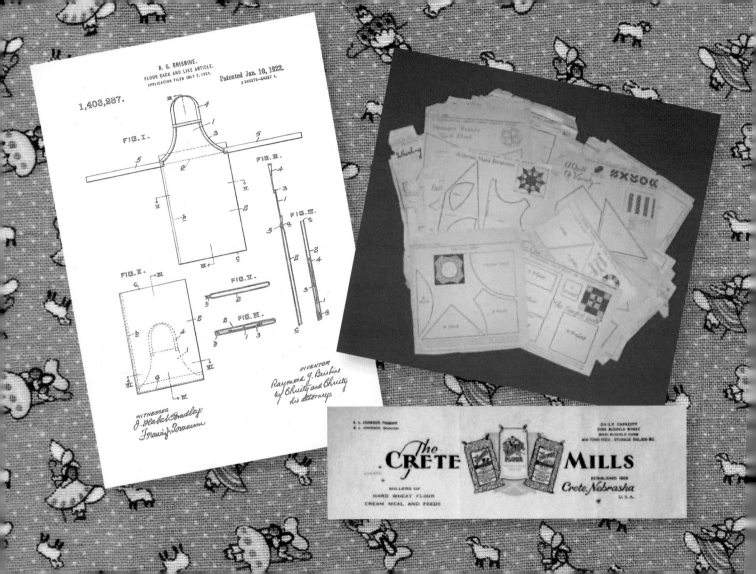

— Chapter Six. —
Feedsack Fill

Bits of information related to flour and feed history were found in the archives. They are too interesting to leave out of the story. I hope you enjoy them as much as I have.

A. W. Guthat of Chicago invented a Sanitary Sack Cleaning Machine in 1918. It used both an air and brush system to remove cement particles, dust, seed, bits of fertilizer and the like from bags that had been returned. The expense and time involved in cleaning and repairing used bags were key factors in the transition to dress print bags.

In the 1925 article, "The Uses of Ex-Flour Sacks," a farm wife from Minnesota eagerly shared advice on practical uses she had found for flour sacks. She made underclothing for the children, pillowcases with crocheted edges, rickrack-trimmed tablecloths, aprons and decorative luncheon cloths with a bluebird in each corner. Her enthusiasm for the cloth was evident in the details provided, including how to remove the ink stamping by soaking overnight in soap and a little kerosene.

A. L. H. Street, writer of the article, added humor with the comment it was easier to find a use for flour sacks than it was to decide "what to do with ex-presidents and old razor blades." In good-natured fun,

Undated letter from A. W. Guthat explaining his machine could thoroughly clean dusty sacks in as little as twenty to thirty minutes. It was patented as a Dusting Apparatus.

The Uses of Ex-Flour Sacks

A COMMUNICATION from a Minnesota farmer's wife to The Farmer, St. Paul, sets in motion numerous practical and unpractical ideas as to what the miller may do to enhance the usefulness of the flour sack after it has served its primary purpose. The communication reads:

"There are ever so many useful things that can be made out of flour sacks. No doubt most housewives have a stack of flour sacks put away somewhere. Most farm women do all of their own baking

"For example, a 98-lb sack could be adapted for use as a chemise for a stout lady, . . . or by making it longer at the expense of narrowness it could be readily converted into a nightie."

and use lots of flour, which enables them to have quite a number of these sacks.

"There are some sacks from which it is hard to remove the paint. On these I put lots of soap and soak them over night and add a little kerosene to the water, and the paint almost always comes out in the first washing. I use the darker ones and those from which the paint will not come off for dish towels. With the frequent washing they soon bleach out white and the paint gradually disappears.

"I find many uses for them. Some I use for underthings for the children, which wear quite well. Others I use for pillow cases on the children's beds, with little edges crocheted on them, and they look very nice. I also have several table cloths made from flour sacks. I take four sacks and fasten them together with rickrack and sew some rickrack around the outside edge.

"I also have a lunch cloth which I made from a large 100-lb sack. I outlined a bluebird in each corner and crocheted a blue edge around it. Slip-on aprons can be made from flour sacks, too, and many other things."

Thus it will be seen that it is by no means as difficult a task to determine what to do with ex-flour sacks as it is to determine what to do with ex-presidents and old razor blades. But the lady from Minnesota does not exhaust all the possibilities of the flour sack, as will appear upon more extended reflection.

The miller should not permit tobacco manufacturers to turn out their product in lunch pails without giving thought to adapting the flour sack to more transient use than delivering milled wheat into the family flour bin. Why not have every flour sack accompanied by a pattern showing what can be made from it? For example, a 98-lb sack could be adapted for use as a chemise for a stout lady, as well as for a table cloth; or by making it longer at the expense of narrowness it could be readily converted into a nightie. A substitution of denim would provide the head of the house with a shirt as well as bread. Smaller sacks could be specially adapted to the making of lingerie of various kinds, with a substitution of silk for cotton in the marketing of high grades of flour. Here, however, the ham packer would have some obvious advantages, should he take the cue.

But the possibilities of the ex-flour sack are by no means limited to bed and table linen and wearing apparel. With a little attention to construction, they can be adapted to uses ranging from containers for tire chains to receptacles for the carrying of a burglar's swag.

The communication above quoted suggests that there is an annoying and unnecessary indelibility of brands on the miller's sacks. Why should the housewife be subjected to the inconvenience of using large quantities of soap and kerosene to eradicate "Smith's Best XXX Flour" from a potential nightgown? An easily erasible ink or paint could be substituted. And it may not be amiss to suggest that edging or embroidery be attached to the top of sacks.

In this connection, the writer cannot avoid recalling that while running a newspaper years ago in Oklahoma Territory a local cotton planter declined to subscribe for the paper on the ground that our "esteemed contemporary's" publication, a six-column folio, was much better adapted to use on pantry shelves than a four-column quarto. As the years pass, our confidence in the judgment of this planter increases.

A. L. H. Street.

"The Uses of Ex-Flour Sacks"
The Northwestern Miller,
October 21, 1925

he offered a few suggestions of his own. Flour should be packaged in denim so the head of the house could wear a new shirt while eating freshly baked bread. He also said while it was true that ex-flour sacks could be used for all sorts of practical wearing apparel, with just a little imagination, they could be converted to hold tire chains or a "burglar's swag."

Not to be outdone by American ingenuity, the paper, *Australasian Baker*, replied that some obvious uses for flour sacks had been overlooked. The first was in the making of a meat safe. First, place the meat on a plate; slip the plate into the sack; tie the top securely and hang it from the porch or a tree. It was suggested the sack have a cylindrical shape so the plate could position snugly against the bottom and avoid the risk of tipping and dripping the contents on the head. Other suggestions were for tent flies and stretchers, to wrap around a tree as a pest deterrent and as "bird frighteners" for pea growers.

Even though the article may have been written in good-natured fun, one can only imagine how it was received by the Minnesota farm wife.

Australian Hints for the Use of Old Flour Sacks

COMMENTING on a recent article in The Northwestern Miller in which A. L. H. Street referred to the suggestions of a farmer's wife for the use of old flour sacks, the Australasian Baker says:

"Waste, we are told, is a terrible thing that saps the strength of the world. If there were no waste at all everybody in the world could work a 22-hour week and have just as much (or as little) wealth as at present and much more time in which to spend it.

"Therefore, let us avoid the waste of used calico flour sacks. Let us invent some methods of using them after they have been emptied of their contents other than for washing the floor or stuffing up cracks in the walls. It should be much easier than finding uses for discarded politicians and safety razor blades."

Continuing, the Australian paper offers a few hints which it considers that the bag manufacturer, baker and miller might do well to consider:

"Our American friend has missed a few of the obvious uses. For instance, he does not include that very popular adaptation of the calico sack so as to make a meat safe. You simply put your meat on a big plate, slip it into the flour sack, tie the top and hang it up on the branch of a tree or from the veranda. The blowflies can buzz around it all day then without doing it any harm. Millers would help here if they would only make the sacks cylindrical, so that the plate would sit better in the bottom. It is distinctly annoying to have a rathe[r] 'gravyfied' piece of meat tip up as o[ne] hangs it over one's head, through th[e] unsuitable nature of the bottom of th[e] sack allowing the plate to slip.

"Nor has he mentioned the great valu[e] of the flour sack for making tent fli[es] and, with the aid of two sapling[s], stretchers. He has entirely overlook[ed] the suitability of the sack for the pu[r]pose of wrapping around a fruit tr[ee] trunk to stop pests crawling up and ea[t]ing the fruit. Millers could help [by] putting a neat little book on the top [of] the sack, thus saving the orchardi[st] much worry. Pea growers find the[m] fine as bird frighteners, but if mille[rs] would only forget their conservatism a[nd] put a few bright splashes of color [on] them they would be much more valuab[le].

"To our mind, however, the great[est] use of all has been forgotten. Every[]body has seen those patterns on cloth [for] 'rag dolls.' Why put the farmer's w[ife] to all this trouble? Why not make [a] few simple adjustments in shape, pr[int] on the outside of the sack the represe[n]tation of a human form, and leave [it] simply to fill it up with grass, chaff, [or] something of the kind, to make a d[oll] for little Mary?

"Some misguided person recently [at]tempted to count the uses of the em[pty] kerosene tin. He died before he co[uld] complete his task. What have mill[ers] been doing to let American oil combi[nes] get such a lead on them?"

"Australian Hints for the Use of Old Flour Sacks"
The Northwestern Miller, May 5, 1926

Raymond G. Brisbine of Dormont, Pennsylvania, filed the application for patent on a flour sack apron on July 7, 1921. Mr. Brisbine was approximately thirty-four years old, a family man and employed as a salesman in a florist store.

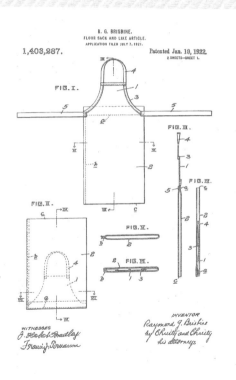

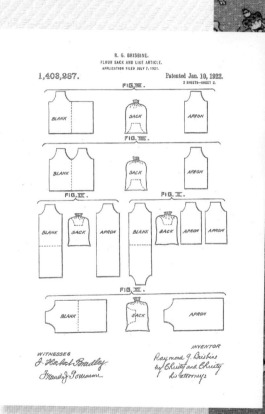

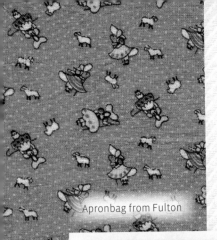

The sack apron appeared again in 1937 under the name "Apronbag" from Fulton Bag & Cotton Mills. It offered "a complete apron, ready to wear when emptied, turned, ripped and washed." The bag was introduced in the January 27, 1937 issue of *The Northwestern Miller* in the article, "Modern Trends in Flour Packaging." It stated, in part,

For some years flour packed in bags made of gingham cloth has been offered the trade by one mill. More recently pastel colored bags have made their appearance, and in one instance at least a feed manufacturer is using this type of bag for packing commercial feeds.

In recent years bag manufacturers have become interested in developing packages that have distinctive merchandising value.

The article went on to explain the importance of *"dressing up a flour package and making it more attractive."* Needlework design imprints and the new apronbag were thought to be a step in the right direction.

Apronbag from Fulton

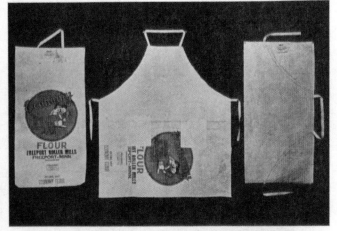

The Fulton "Apronbag." On left is bag; tape is inside and does not show when bag is filled. Illustration on right shows bag turned inside out, with stenciling for pockets and for form-fitting cutting if so desired. In middle is completed apron. If consumer does not want cut-out apron, all she has to do is rip stitching on side and bottom of bag, launder, and full-sized apron is ready for use.

"Sack of Oats Saves Life As Man Falls Off Cliff"

Frank Domikoski, an employee of a feed company in Pennsylvania, was delivering a sack of oats when he slipped on a narrow path and slid down a hill. The sack lodged against a tree and kept Mr. Domikoski from tumbling the rest of the way down the cliff. He suffered a fractured hip in the fall.

SACK OF OATS SAVES LIFE AS MAN FALLS OFF CLIFF

PITTSBURGH, PA.—A sack of oats, which, lodging against a tree, arrested the fall of Frank Domikoski, as he tumbled down a 300-ft embankment, saved that man's life on Jan. 15. Mr. Domikoski, an employee of the F. R. Patterson Feed Co., was delivering the sack of oats, which he carried on his shoulder, when he lost his footing while walking on a narrow pathway along the side of a steep hill. He clung to his burden as he fell, and when the sack lodged against a tree, 15 feet down the side of the hill, Mr. Domikoski shouted for help. He was rescued by passers-by, who formed a human chain to retrieve him. A fractured hip was the extent of his injury.

The Northwestern Miller
January 20, 1926

Game front and back with the trademark Ceresota Boy slicing bread from his bench

Some millers gave needle books to customers. This one advertises Mother's Best Flour "for better bread, rolls and pastry." The Sharp & Son needles are still in perfect condition.

This undated Ceresota Flour Numerical Mind Reader game was likely a promotional item. The instructions read:

These cards are numbered from 1 to 8. Place card No. 1 with "Up" at the top. Show card No. 2 to the person whose age you wish to find, and ask if the number representing that person's age is on the card. If it is, lay card No. 2 on card No. 1 with "YES" at the top. If it is not, lay "NO" at the top. Repeat this process with each card in regular order. The correct number will show on the other side. These cards will correctly tell any age from 1 to 99.

If the instructions are followed carefully, it does, indeed, tell the correct age.

This letterhead from The Crete Mills of Crete, Nebraska, is dated October 9, 1930.

A second Crete Mills letterhead is dated January 25, 1934.

"MISS VITALITY" GOES TO ENGLAND

* * *   * * *

But Her Trip Is Made for Business Not Pleasure

MISS VITALITY, the wheat flour salesgirl, is visiting in England. The fame of the "vitality girl," whose portrait was used in advertisements put out by the Wheat Flour Institute, Chicago, has spread to the United Kingdom. The portrait of this young lady, which appeared in THE NORTHWESTERN MILLER last spring, attracted the attention of the committee of the British Bread Advertising Campaign and steps were taken to secure permission from the Wheat Flour Institute to use it as a basis for advertisements in the Bread Advertising Campaign in Great Britain. The permission was readily given and the attractive figure of the young lady is now adorning national newspaper advertising and bill posters in Britain. The vitality girl poster is regarded as one of the most successful that so far has been used in the British campaign. The accompanying slogan is: "Eat Bread for Energy!"

Pictured at the right is the vitality girl poster as used by the Wheat Flour Institute in bread promotional advertising

in the United States. In private life, the model is Miss Jolieta McCready, Chicago radio player and advertising model. Recently she has been appearing on sustaining radio programs over station WAAF.

I WANT TO KEEP MY VITALITY

I eat **HOT BISCUITS** FOR FOOD ENERGY

"Miss Vitality" Goes to England
The Northwestern Miller,
November 25, 1936

In 1935, the Wheat Flour Institute planned to increase sales by selecting a beautiful, vivacious woman to symbolize the health benefits obtained from including their product in the daily diet. Miss Jolieta McCready won the title of "Miss Vitality" and became identified with the saying, "I want to keep my vitality. I eat hot biscuits for food energy." She proved to be so popular in the states, permission was sought to use her in advertisements for Great Britain's Bread Advertising Campaign.

Fleischmann sponsored a radio program called "The Bakers' Broadcast" to "help increase consumption of baked goods." Regulars were host Feg Murray, Ozzie Nelson and His Orchestra and Harriet Hilliard. Famous screen stars were guests of the show, which aired every Sunday beginning October 3, 1937.

Hollywood movie stars helped boost sales of "Tested Quality doughnuts" for the baking industry. Full-page, color advertisements appeared in the Saturday Evening Post and Life starting in September of 1938. Thirty-seven newspapers ran the ads in their Sunday editions every other week for one year. Milling periodicals were also used.

STAR-STUDDED ENTERTAINMENT

featuring

FEG MURRAY, OUTSTANDING AUTHORITY ON HOLLYWOOD! INSIDE FACTS ABOUT THE STARS! FAMOUS SCREEN FAVORITES in PERSON!

An industry program— sponsored by Fleischmann to help increase consumption of Baked Goods

and those nationwide favorites OZZIE NELSON and HARRIET HILLIARD

Nothing Like the NEW "BAKERS' BROADCAST" Has Ever Been Presented!

It's on the way—a great new "Bakers' Broadcast" to thrill America! It's different...it's amazing...it's sure-fire! And it starts Sunday, October 3, direct from Hollywood.

Feg Murray's famous "Seein' Stars" cartoon is widely syndicated in newspapers read by millions of people throughout the country. Now Fleischmann brings Feg Murray in person for the first time, in dramatic presentations of inside facts about filmland's great.

Each week, Feg Murray will present famous screen favorites as his guests...

names known round the world...box-office personalities...idols of millions of movie fans. All America will tune in to hear Feg Murray and screenland's headliners. "Seein' Stars" is bound to make "The Bakers' Broadcast" more popular than ever.

In response to popular demand, Ozzie Nelson and His Orchestra and Harriet Hilliard will also be on the program every week. Get set for the new and greater "Bakers' Broadcast," on the air for bakers starting October 3, and every Sunday thereafter.

Ozzie and Harriet join "Bakers' Broadcast"
The Northwestern Miller and *American Baker*, October 6, 1937

Olivia De Havilland, Pat O'Brien, Margaret Lindsay
and Dick Powell help boost sales.
The Northwestern Miller and *American Baker,* August 3, 1938

Test Begins on New Merchandising Kit for Resale of Dress Print Bags

The first of a national series of tests on a new merchandising kit for once-used dress print bags began Oct. 4 in Beaumont, Texas. The plan has been in the research stage for almost a year.

The advertising firm of R. F. Nylen & Associates, Chicago, creators of the patented and copyrighted merchandising plan, is staging the test in co-operation with the purchasing and merchandising departments of the Tayster Bread Co.'s new plant in Beaumont.

The new "completed package" idea is based on a complete merchandising program. In cooperation with various trade associations and their members, Nylen & Associates launched several hundred basic interviews. The final plan now in action is the answer to interviews with bakers, grocers, food store operators and the housewife.

"Sales research showed," it is reported by the advertising firm, "that once you enter any city trading area you encounter a psychological mental block if too much emphasis is laid on the word 'bags.' It is unfortunate that this word has too many unfavorable connotations. You may say 'cotton sacking.' But the phrase that outsells all others is 'matching dress print cotton sacking.'"

The first problem was the selection of patterns and colors. Design material that is to be offered in dress print textiles to bag manufacturers is sampled by showing each pattern in each color combination to 2,000 women. This routine check is made periodically.

"Some bakers are already ordering bags directly from the bag manufacturers and have them shipped to the millers," Nylen & Associates reports. "Plans are now formulating whereby the baker can ask the miller to provide shipments of flour in certain code number patterns, according to swatch samples. Once ordered, duplicate swatches are sent to Nylen & Associates who will provide the matching buttons and thread, and all promotional material."

The promotional kit is based primarily on four matching empty flour containers which have a total yardage of four and two thirds yards. Eight harmonizing buttons and matching thread are enclosed in a heat-sealed cellophane envelope which goes into the kit. To complete the kit a special edition of a cotton dress pattern book that has had over 3 million copies distributed in the last few years was revised and issued under the title, "21 New Patterns."

Kit Sells as Unit

The final step in the kit was the design of an 11x14 in. heavy cellophane envelope designed to sell the kit as a unit. Printed in three colors — royal blue, persimmon orange and white — it suggests sewing activity, titled, "Your New Wardrobe." With plenty of open space, the design of the cloth is very apparent.

A poster for bakeries and food stores has also been designed.

DRESS PRINT KIT—Shown above is the complete dress print kit to be sold to housewives through retail outlets. Four matching printed flour containers in cloth are enclosed in a cellophane envelope. In a small envelope, enclosed in the larger one, is a spool of matching thread and eight specially-designed buttons. A new pattern book completes the merchandising package.

...cluded is an inventory control system to make sure all kits reach the stores complete, and instructions on how to package these kits at the bakery.

"Test Begins on New Merchandising Kit for Resale of Dress Print Bags"
The Northwestern Miller, October 12, 1948

SPORTS SHIRTS FROM COTTON BAGS—The Chase Bag Co. bowling team shown here is wearing bowling shirts made from the company's "Pretty-Print" cotton flour and feed bags. According to J. H. Counce, Chase branch manager, the new sports fashion first came into use with the sponsoring of bowling teams during the 1947-48 season by bakers whose flour came packed in printed cotton sacks. Following that, Mr. Counce pointed out, bag patterns began to be used by softball teams, golfers, and other sports enthusiasts.

The Chase Bag Co. bowling team wore shirts made from Chase Pretty-Prints. Other sports teams did the same.
Feedstuffs, October 9, 1948

The new "twin-towl bag" from the Pioneer Bag Company of North Kansas City, Missouri, combined a Turkish towel and a tea towel. *Feedstuffs*, December 16, 1950

On October 4, 1948, testing began in Beaumont, Texas, on a "new merchandising kit for once-used dress print bags." The prints were selected based on the favorites chosen by a panel of 2000 women. Each kit included four matching dress print flour sacks, eight buttons, matching thread and the dress pattern book, "*21 New Patterns*." All items were enclosed in a heavy cellophane envelope with the colorful label "Your New Wardrobe!" printed in royal blue, persimmon orange and white.

Southern Flour Mills of Albemarle, North Carolina, sold their product in these Fulton bags with doll backprints. One has "Sailor Boy" on the cap and the other says only "Dress Doll" on the body. The age and other details are unknown, but aren't they sweet?

Another mystery doll backprint is "Kiddy Kut-Outs" by the Millhiser Bag Co. of Richmond, Virginia.

These mystery sacks include the pattern pieces and instructions for making various doll clothes. Some of the clothing styles were available in different prints and colors. They have the typical thread tracks around the edges and measure about 20" x 18". The clothing style appears to date to around the 1960s. Whether the sacks are vintage is questionable. Several have the letter "P" along the lower edge.

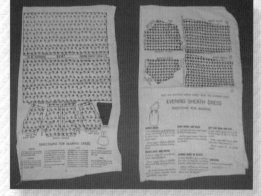

Gingham Girl Flour was sold for many years. This paper label came from Gingham Girl Stone Ground Whole Wheat Flour. It contains a zip code which indicates a date of 1963 or later.

A Team: Feedsacks and Kansas City Star Patterns

Two favorites with quilters are the *Kansas City Star* quilt patterns and feedsacks. Both were immensely popular during the same time period. *The Kansas City Star* began its famous 1000+ quilt pattern series on September 19, 1928, with the printing of the patchwork pattern, "Pine Tree," and concluded its run on May 24, 1961, with "A Fan of Many Colors."

The first dress print bags were available to the public shortly before April 15, 1925. Some three decades with thousands of delightful prints followed before the reign of the lowly dress print bag ended.

It seems appropriate that both the KC Star patterns and colorfully printed feedsacks are popular once again and high on the wish list of many collectors.

NET WEIGHT
STONE GROUND
WHOLE WHEAT FLOUR

GINGHAM GIRL ®

"The World's Finest"
STONE GROUND
WHOLE WHEAT FLOUR

BAKING QUALITY GUARANTEED BY
DIXIE-PORTLAND FLOUR MILLS, INC.   MEMPHIS, TENNESSEE 38187

Kansas City Star newspaper pattern clippings

Feedsacks in vibrant colors and patterns

Bibliography

Chapter One

The Washington Post, "Farewell to the Old Flour Sack," April 28, 1922

Bob Ausbourne, Genealogist

Ancestry.com

Missouri State Archives

U.S. Patent and Trademark Office, Publication Number: 01611403

W. G. Martin, Jr., "Gingham Is Used for Flour Sacks," *The Northwestern Miller*, April 15, 1925, pg. 226

Advertisements by Geo. P. Plant Milling Co., *The Northwestern Miller*, June 3, 1925, pg. 928-929; June 10, 1925, pg. 1029

Wayne G. Martin, Jr., A. S. Purves and S. O. Werner, "The Associated Bakers of America at St. Louis," *The American Baker*, May 26, 1926, page 766-768

Loris Connolly, "Recycling Feed Sacks and Flour Bags: Thrifty Housewives or Marketing Success Story?" *Dress*, Volume 19, 1992

Virginia Gunn, "The Gingham Dog or the Calico Cat: Grassroots Quilts of the Early Twentieth Century," *Uncoverings 2007: Volume 28 of the Research Papers of the American Quilt Study Group*

Montgomery Ward & Co. Catalogs, 1923; 1925. Pages used with permission of Midwest Catalog Brands, Inc. Montgomery Ward and Wards are registered marks of Midwest Catalog Brands, Inc.

Chapter 2

Worster, Donald, *Dust Bowl: The Southern Plains in the 1930s*, Oxford University Press, USA, 2004, pages 113-114

Nathoo, Tasnim, et. al, "An Analysis of the Development of Canadian Food Fortification Policies: The Case of Vitamin B," Oxford Journals, Volume 20, Number 4, pages 375-382, Health Promotion International, Oxford University Press, November 12, 2005

Percy Kent Bag Company, Inc., *PK: Our First Hundred Years*, undated booklet, pages 6-7

Dinsmore, Gertrude Allen, "Sackcloth Up-To-Date," *Los Angeles Times*, February 22, 1942

Fowler, Gene and Crawford, Bill, *Border Radio: Quacks, Yodelers, Pitchmen, Psychics, and Other Amazing Broadcasters of the American Airwaves*, University of Texas Press, 2002 Revised

Kaylakie, Marcia, *Texas Quilts and Quilters: A Lone Star Legacy*, Texas Tech University Press, 2007

Time, "Flour Salesman," July 25, 1938

Time, "O'Daniel Pays His Tithe," April 29, 1940

Rhoades, Ruth, *Feed Sacks in Georgia*, Morris Publishing, 2006

Online sources:

{Ed. note: Online addresses are subject to change and sometimes disappear completely.}

Trew, Delbert, "Dust Bowl Was Deadly," http://www.texasescapes.com/DelbertTrew/Dust-Bowl-was-deadly.htm

Larry O'Dell, "Poultry Industry," Encyclopedia of Oklahoma History and Culture , http://digital.library.okstate.edu/encyclopedia (accessed March 11, 2009)

"Surviving the Dust Bowl," http://www.pbs.org/wgbh/amex/dustbowl/

U. S. Department of Agriculture, http://www.ers.usda.gov/

VanGiezen, Robert and Schwenk, Albert E., "Compensation from Before World War I Through the Great Depression," Bureau of Labor Statistics, www.bls.gov/

Bemis, "1930 - 1939, New Products and Locations Flourish," http://www.bemis150.com/content/timeline.asp

Werthan Packaging, Inc., http://www.werthan.com/wpihistory.htm

Handbook of Texas Online, s.v. "," http://www.tshaonline.org/handbook/online/articles/WW/xgw1.html (accessed March 11, 2009)

Handbook of Texas Online, s.v. "," http://www.tshaonline.org/handbook/online/articles/OO/fo'4.html (accessed March 11, 2009)

Hughes, Patrick, L., "Only in Texas: Ma, Pa, and Pappy," http://www2.austin.cc.tx.us/lpatrick/his1693/mapa.htm

"W. Lee O'Daniel and His Hillbilly Boys!," The Old Radio Times, February 2008, Number 27, pages 13-18, http://www.otrr.org/FILES/Times_Archive_pdf/2008_02Feb.pdf

"Border Radio," The Old Radio Times, February 2008, Number 27, pages 19-23, http://www.otrr.org/FILES/Times_Archive_pdf/2008_02Feb.pdf

Old Time Radio Researchers Group, http://www.otrr.org/

Pourade, Richard F., "The History of San Diego," https://www.sandiegohistory.org/books/pourade/rising/risingchapter4.htm

Amero, Richard, "History of the Casa del Prado Building in Balboa Park," https://www.sandiegohistory.org/bpbuildings/casaprad.htm

"Balboa Park History, Notes, 1935, California-Pacific International Exposition -
1935, The New York Times Index," https://www.sandiegohistory.org/amero/notes-1935new.htm

"California Pacific Exposition San Diego 1935-1936, Chapter Three: Exposition Exhibits," https://www.sandiegohistory.org/calpac/35expoh3.htm

Chapter 3

"They Made Their Dresses Out of Bags," Feedstuffs, December 6, 1941, page 20

"WPB Rule Restricts Size of Feed Bags," Feedstuffs, January 16, 1943, page 7

Goodwin, Doris Kearns, No Ordinary Time: Franklin and Eleanor Roosevelt: The Home Front in World War II, Simon and Schuster, 1995, page 355

Hill, Daniel Delis, As Seen in Vogue: A Century of American Fashion in Advertising, Texas Tech University Press, 2007, pages 70-71

Kansas City Times, May 12, 1945

Cook, Anna Lue, Identification & Value Guide to Textile Bags, Books Americana, Inc., 1990

Lingren, Wilfred E., "Glamor Comes to the Cotton Bag," Feedstuffs, August 24, 1946, pages 34-37

"Decisive Farm Vote: Why Men on Tractors Wanted Truman," Newsweek, November 15, 1948, page 25

"Introduce New Bag," Feedstuffs, May 21, 1949, page 6

"Pullet Poll Gives Edge to Truman," Feedstuffs, September 4, 1948, page 38

"Staley Poll Picks the Winner," Feedstuffs, November 6, 1948, page 1

McGinnis, Edie, Beautiful Quilts from Humble Beginnings, Kansas City Star Books, 2006

Online sources:

{Ed. note: Online sources are subject to change and sometimes disappear completely.}

Agricultural Experiment Station, Kansas State College of Agriculture and Applied Science, Manhattan, Kansas, In Cooperation with United States Weather Bureau, September 1942, Bulletin 302, pages 13, 14:

http://www.oznet.k-state.edu/historicpublications/pubs/SB302.PDF

Kansas Climate Collection, Climate of Kansas, pages 119-127, http://www.ksre.ksu.edu/wdl/climate/

"Foreign Affairs: Franklin D. Roosevelt, 32nd President," American Experience, The Presidents, http://www.pbs.org/wgbh/amex/presidents/32_f_roosevelt/f_roosevelt_foreign.html

"Allied Powers (World War II)," New World Encyclopedia, http://www.newworldencyclopedia.org/entry/Allied_Powers

"Timeline of the Great Depression," http://www.pbs.org/wgbh/amex/rails/timeline/index.html

"American Fashion Goes to War" American Decades. The Gale Group, Inc. 2001. Encyclopedia.com. (March 27, 2009), http://www.encyclopedia.com/doc/1G2-3468301492.html

"Milestones in United Nations History," http://www.un.org/Overview/milesto4.htm

Harry S. Truman Library & Museum, http://www.trumanlibrary.org/index.php

"Dave Leip's Atlas of U.S. Presidential Elections," http://www.uselectionatlas.org/RESULTS/national.php?f=0&year=1948

"Presidential Politics," American Experience, http://www.pbs.org/wgbh/amex/truman/sfeature/sf_ppolitics.html

Chapter 5

"Speedy Change," (photo: luncheon cloth), *Feedstuffs*, August 19, 1950, page 11

Percy Kent Bag Company, Inc., PK: *Our First Hundred Years*, undated booklet, page 9

Online Sources:

{*Ed. note: Online sources are subject to change and sometimes disappear completely.*}

"America on the Move," National Museum of American History, http://americanhistory.si.edu/onthemove/collection/object_613.html

"The Kaiser," Second Chance Garage, http://www.secondchancegarage.com/public/319.cfm

1949-1953 Kaiser Traveler and Vagabond, Auto Editors of Consumer Guide, http://auto.howstuffworks.com/1949-1953-kaiser-traveler-vagabond.htm

"Dapper Little Bird," *The Deseret News*, Feb 9, 1950, http://news.google.com/newspapers?id=F0IOAAAAIBAJ&sjid=0H8DAAAAIBAJ&pg=5297,1598926&dq=dapper-little-bird

"Werthan Bag History," http://www.werthan.com/wpihistory.htm

"*1880 - 1890, Incorporation and the Beginnings of Expansion,*" http://www.bemis150.com/content/timeline.asp

"1950 - 1959, The Progress of Plastic," http://www.bemis150.com/content/timeline.asp

"1930 - 1939, New Products and Locations Flourish," http://www.bemis150.com/content/timeline.asp

Chapter 6

U.S. Patent and Trademark Office, Publication Number: 01298933

A. L. H. Street, "The Uses of Ex-Flour Sacks," *The*

Northwestern Miller, October 21, 1925, page 247

"Australian Hints for the Use of Old Flour Sacks," *The Northwestern Miller*, May 5, 1926, page 471

U.S. Patent and Trademark Office, Publication Number: 01403287

Heritage Quest Online, 1920 Federal Census

Martin, Wayne G. Jr., "Modern Trends in Flour Packaging," *The Northwestern Miller*, January 27, 1937, pages 40-43

Sack of Oats Saves Life as Man Falls Off Cliff, *The Northwestern Miller*, January 20, 1926, page 233

"Miss Vitality" Goes to England, *The Northwestern Miller*, November 25, 1936, page 505

"Star-Studded Entertainment" advertisement, *The Northwestern Miller* and *American Baker*, October 6, 1937, pages 48 and 49

"Doughnuts Are Starred in Hollywood," *The Northwestern Miller* and *American Baker*, August 3, 1938, pages 19-22

"Test Begins on New Merchandising Kit for Resale of Dress Print Bags," *The Northwestern Miller*, October 12, 1948, page 18

Google Patent Search, http://www.google.com/patents, http://www.google.com/patents?id=y7NDAAAAEBAJ&dq=1403287